Wishing you a Merry Christmas
and a Happy New Year Ac
the Directors of Caprice Ho

JESUR

December 2003

# simple ways to success

# wine

## Susy Atkins

photography by William Reavell

This edition first published in 2003 by Quadrille Publishing Limited
Alhambra House  27-31 Charing Cross Road  London WC2H OLS

**Editorial director** Jane O'Shea  **Creative director** Helen Lewis
**Project editor** Lisa Pendreigh  **Designers** Jim Smith and Anne Wilson
**Photographer** William Reavell  **Food stylist** Angela Boggiano  **Props stylist** Jane Campsie
**Production** Vincent Smith and Jane Rogers

Cataloguing in Publication Data: a catalogue record for this book is available from the British Library.

ISBN 1 84400 072 9
Printed in China

# contents

# introduction

Never before have so many people been interested in wine. Nowadays, wine is cherished by adults from all walks of life – male or female, young or old. We adore not only expensive bottles of claret, but everyday wines from all corners of the world. This is partly because quality has improved vastly over the past twenty years. Cheap wine used to be awful stuff: badly made, faintly grubby and often horribly sweet. How lucky we are now to have great wines crowding our shops. Not everything is superb, of course, but general standards have soared. Then there's the increased availability of decent wines. Retailers have done much to make buying wine easy; just peruse the extensive shelves and sling a bottle in with the weekly shop. It's a far cry from when the meek had to pluck up the courage to enter the hallowed portals of a venerable wine merchant!

Yet, wine is still seen by some as mystifying, even intimidating. This is a shame. True, it is a complicated subject to grasp. Today there are so many styles of wine, grape varieties, new regions and techniques, that trying to find out more can seem daunting. Much easier, then, to stick to one brand, one grape variety, one price point. But how boring, as well. To me, that's like cooking the same dish every night or reading the same book over and over again. We don't spend our entire lives eating spag bol and reading holiday blockbusters, so why stick to 'identikit' wines? It really *is* worth getting to know more about wine – a little knowledge does go a very long way here. You will get a whole heap of pleasure from the flavours you discover as a result. Who knows? It may start you on a whole new adventure: finding dishes to match your wines, travelling to wine regions around the world, making new friends with the same interest… If not, well, isn't it worth giving your taste buds a refreshing wake-up-call?

This book makes learning about wine an enjoyable experience. It is organised into three sections: an introduction to the subject and the factors that influence the liquid in our glasses; a central part focusing on the ten key styles of wine; and finally a useful summary of how to serve, store, order and match it with food. There is some subjectivity in categorising wines by style. Rioja, I decided, is generally not a big, powerful red, but medium-bodied and soft. You may disagree – and that's your prerogative. Likewise, it's impossible to avoid the odd generalisation. Not *all* Merlots are the same, by any means, so although this popular grape variety mainly appears in the section on 'Medium-bodied, Soft Reds', there are also references to it within 'Light and Smooth Reds' and even in the 'Full-bodied Reds' section. That said, this method of grouping wines by style, according to their weight, richness, dryness, flavour spectrum and natural food partners, is more useful to the relative beginner than trawling through the world of wine, country by country, like a geography lesson.

A final word on the recommendations given for each style. In my view, these are some of the most consistently impressive and interesting producers of the wines described. They are not comprehensive lists of the top bottles, but simply some labels that will give you a good start. My recommendations vary a great deal; one might be a fine, expensive wine, while another is good value – but there are many, many other examples available. Where a style of wine is especially reliable from supermarket own-label ranges (such as sherry or South African Chenin Blanc), I have said so. Look out for those I recommend, but find your own wines, too. Get tasting. It is the only way to pin down your own likes and dislikes and should be practised at every opportunity – hardly a strain!

# 1 the basics

# what is wine?

Wine is fermented grape juice. It can be hard to bear in mind this simple fact when reading dozens of pages crammed full of other information on the subject. But it's quite straightforward – if you leave a load of crushed grapes in a container in warmish conditions, the natural yeasts will get to work on the fruit, turning the sugars into alcohol. Strain this pippy mess, and the end result is a liquid that could be called wine. Pretty horrible wine, it should be said, but wine nonetheless. There's nothing particularly magical about any of that, but what I find fascinating is the amazing range of flavours, textures and aromas that is produced in such liquids. What, exactly, makes an elegant Sauvignon Blanc produced in France's Loire Valley such a different creature from a thick red Syrah made in the Rhône Valley? For that matter, why does the Loire white have a different flavour from a Sauvignon Blanc produced in New Zealand? Or – and this is where wine gets most intriguing, or nerdy, depending on your level of interest – why is Pouilly-Fumé, a Sauvignon Blanc from Pouilly-sur-Loire, different from one made a few miles away in Sancerre? Or even from the one made at the neighbour's vineyard across the road? Why do wines evolve differently over time?

I'm beginning to sound like a three-year-old with all these questions, but happily there are answers to each one (as you will discover as you read on). Clearly, many factors influence the taste of the liquid in your wineglass. The most important of these are the grape varieties and blends of grapes used – Chardonnay, Cabernet Sauvignon, Merlot and so on (which is the subject of Part Two) – the region where they are grown, its climate and its soil, the conditions of a particular year (vintage), and, of course, the winemakers themselves and the decisions they bring to bear on grape-growing, harvesting, vinification and oak-ageing. There's quite a lot to get to grips with, so these first pages provide a general introduction to all these subjects and more. Once you realise just how many natural factors and human decisions affect the making of wine, it's clear to see why there is a such a wide range of styles available, and why certain wines taste a certain way.

Let's go back to that basic fact: that wine is simply fermented grape juice. One part of the winemaking process that is seldom discussed is the work of yeast. In the past, wild, native yeast was always the natural force that fermented the fruit. In the modern era, strains of super-efficient, pure yeasts are cultivated especially to ensure consistency and reduce the chances of spoilage. Some highly respected winemakers, even those working in high-tech, progressive winemaking regions, have started to reject these strains and return to wild yeast. Their complaint is that cultivated yeasts lead to uniform flavours in wine – especially if they are used the world over, perhaps reducing somewhat the regional characteristics of different natural yeast. It is true that native yeast can contribute a 'wilder', more pronounced, even spicy flavour to a wine, but this only works with certain *cuvées* (blend or batch of wine) – others suit the subtler, even effect of cultivated yeast. A canny winemaker should know which type of yeast to employ for each wine produced. At least the choice is there.

Then there's the matter of leaving a fermented wine on its dead yeast sediment, the lees, which sounds a bit unpleasant, like using a mouldy loaf to make breadcrumbs. In fact, this lees-ageing can be an important element in some wines; the liquid picks up some creamy, doughy, biscuity flavour and aroma from the sediment before being racked off and bottled. The words *sur lie* on a French label indicate a wine that has been lees-aged for longer than usual.

The lees are sometimes even stirred into the wine at regular intervals (a process called *bâtonnage*) to impart even more yeasty, bready flavour. In southern Spain, yeast plays an important part in the sherry-making, too, forming a thick natural blanket on top of a wine as it sits in a barrel, protecting it from air and imparting its own bready, fresh tang to the wine. This coating, called *flor*, forms naturally in the sherry towns of Jerez, Sanlúcar de Barrameda and Puerto de la Santa María, which lie close to the coast, and it helps to form this unique and wonderful style of wine. Did I say there was nothing magical about the natural process of yeast working on grapes? It suddenly sounds pretty amazing, after all.

We tend to divide wine into three groups according to colour: white, red or rosé. In fact, rosé wines, which can range from the deepest, richest cerise (more like a light red) to the palest tinge of pink possible (more like a white), fill in the palette between white and red. White wines are usually made from white grapes, but occasionally the clear juice of red grapes is run off and fermented; the skins are not crushed, obviously, as that would colour the juice. This is common practice in sparkling winemaking, where the red grape Pinot Noir is often used to make white fizz. Look out for the words *blanc de noirs* on a label to indicate a clear sparkler made from red grapes.

Rosé is usually created by leaving the juice and skins of red grapes to macerate together for a short time before running off the light pink juice and fermenting it separately. For more discussion of this, see the section on 'Rosés' in Part Two (see pages 120–129). The majority of red wine is made by crushing black grapes and allowing them to ferment together so that plenty of colour, flavour and tannin leaches into the wine. The solid matter floats on top of the liquid, and sometimes winemakers deliberately press this 'cap' back down again and again into the juice to help extract more character from the skin.

A few lighter, softer reds, notably Beaujolais, are produced in a different way – the grapes are not crushed, but gradually ferment and burst, which leads to a less tannic, juicier style of wine.

Visit most modern wineries and you will see a regiment of sparkling-clean stainless-steel tanks where the wine is fermented. It's highly likely you will also see a barrel room. The use of oak barrels to ferment and/or age wine – a process which gives the liquid a distinctive woody character, either subtle or overt – is widespread. Used carefully, oak maturation can add layers of complexity and depth of flavour to a wine. There's more discussion of oak relating to specific styles of wine in other parts of this book.

The age of a wine is another highly important factor. Most bottles are filled, shipped, sold and consumed in a matter of months (even weeks) after harvest – and often they are enjoyed for their youthful vibrancy. But some wines are meant to be opened when they are older. You might buy a bottle of young claret or vintage port or fine German Riesling (three types of wine that repay cellaring) and decide to keep it for several years before opening so it is more mellow and easy-drinking. Other wines are aged before you buy them; Rioja *reserva* is a good example, as it is traditionally matured at the *bodega* (winery) in Spain before release and so is ready to drink when bought. Whatever you do, drink up your wine soon after opening the bottle. It is a fragile liquid that is ruined by exposure to air. Think of the way fruit turns brown when you cut into it; wine is the same. Oxidised, it ain't nice – so never keep a bottle for more than three or four days unless it's destined for the cooking pot.

Those are some of the basic facts about wine, which are all expanded on at length further on in this book. But let's cut to a popular question about wine that many will want answered from the start. Why is some of it wretchedly expensive, when many bottles cost relatively little? It does seem hard to understand why a Chardonnay from Eastern Europe is one-tenth the price of a Chardonnay from a vineyard in Burgundy. I'd love to be able to state categorically that the more pricey bottles always taste much, much better, but that simply isn't the case. They tend to, but we have all had the sorry experience of opening a supposedly fine bottle and being disappointed. Expensive wine is expensive for one or more of the following reasons: a) because it comes from a small restricted area and demand for the tiny amount of wine made there is high – the basic economics of supply and demand; b) if it is made in a part of the world where costs are high, as opposed to an area where grapes and labour come cheap; c) if the grape varieties used are expensive, perhaps from low-yielding vines or in an area where there are restrictions on how much fruit is produced; d) if the wine/winery/winemaker is particularly fashionable or has been rated highly by an influential critic; e) if it is the product of a fine vintage in a region where such things matter.

But who cares about all that, apart from wine snobs? I'll let you into a secret: many true wine buffs drink inexpensive wines as well as the odd luxury label. That's because they know enough about the stuff to look beyond the obvious, and they can pluck out a bargain. If you find a wine – cheap or expensive – that you like and which suits your budget, then go for it. Don't be bamboozled into buying fancy labels with terrifying price tags for the sake of it.

## Organic wines

There is currently more interest in organic wine than ever before. Organic wine is made from the same grapes in exactly the same way as ordinary wine, but without the use of chemicals – herbicides, fungicides, pesticides, artificial fertilisers – in the vineyard or the winery. In short, organic wine is made from organic grapes. Less sulphur is used to preserve the bottled wine as well. This doesn't mean that you won't get a hangover – organic wine still contains normal levels of alcohol – but it's worth trying an organic bottle if you suspect you may be allergic to sulphur or trace elements of chemicals. It is definitely good news for the health of the vines, the land and the local wildlife if organic viticulture is practised.

You can find organic wine in any major wine shop or supermarket nowadays, but unfortunately it isn't always clearly labelled. A symbol from The Soil Association is a good clue. The price for organic wine tends to be slightly higher, because growing grapes organically is more expensive and labour intensive than using chemicals. Quality is as varied for organic wine as it is for non-organic wine: expect some great wines, many ordinary ones, as well as a few duds.

# climate

Have you ever wondered why the cooler far northern regions rarely make palatable red wine? They can manage decent whites and sparklers, honest, but the reds remain on the stalky, thin side. It's because of their cool climate. There just isn't enough hot sun for black grapes to ripen sufficiently. Now and again, in a very warm year, the grapes from a particularly sheltered spot make the grade, but most of the time, the winemakers can forget it.

Climate matters. Even in areas that consistently produce premium wines, the style is dictated by the local temperature and rainfall. Heat ripens grapes, making them sweeter, so that more sugar is available to turn into alcohol during fermentation. That's why wines from hot climates tend to be richer and headily alcoholic, whereas wines from cool climates are lighter in strength. Vineyards that don't get enough sun produce poor wines, and reds in particular can suffer from a green, stalky character. New Zealand used to have this problem with many of its reds, and one solution has been to choose warmer sites for some grape varieties.

This is not to say that warmer climates always produce the best wines. Well-handled grapes from somewhat cooler spots retain a fresh acidity, and can make more crisp and elegant wines. Although the big, powerful bottles from warm countries became very fashionable in the late twentieth century, winemakers – and increasingly, wine drinkers – are now recognising that wines with more balance and finesse sometimes come not from baking-hot vineyards but from sites where the sun's warmth is tempered by cool, maritime breezes, or where there is a significant drop in night-time temperatures. That cool, night-time drop in temperature is perhaps one of the most important factors in growing decent grapes for wine. Warm, sunny days create ripeness, and cool nights help retain acidity and fresh aromas in grapes. It's impossible to imagine a wine as wonderfully subtle and complex as Mosel's Riesling being produced in a warmer part of the world. Cooler parts of California and Australia, South Africa and Chile are being sought out in order to get better-quality grapes. In warmer winemaking areas – say, Stellenbosch in the Cape – some of the best vineyards are planted up the hillsides as higher altitude means cooler conditions.

But let's not write off the exceedingly hot spots, either. If a rich, strapping style of red is wanted, and the grape varieties planted are suitable for this climate, then hot sun can give exactly the required result. Think of Châteauneuf-du-Pape in France's Rhône Valley, celebrated for tannic, concentrated reds. These are made in a very warm region from red grapes that need lots of sun to ripen properly, and the result is powerfully alcoholic, dark, ripe wines.

Likewise, Australia's hot Barossa Valley makes impressive, hearty Shirazes that are admired the world over. An Australian red from a cooler part of the country, such as the Yarra Valley in Victoria, simply has a different, more restrained character. As long as winemakers know what they are doing, and bring their expertise to bear on these different climates, then *vive la différence*!

There are various techniques grape-growers use to get the required ripeness in their fruit. Leaf plucking is one; greenery around the bunches is removed so that the grapes sit in the sun, not the shade. Separating the vine's canopy and tying it back on a trellis (a bit like creating a parting in the hair) exposes the grapes, too. I've even seen white sheeting at the base of a vine to reflect the sun's rays up onto the fruit. Then again, those working in very hot areas have to watch out for burning on their grapes (keep some of those leaves/canopy to shade the fruit)... It's all about managing the conditions nature has given, in order to get the results required.

**Above** The warm Barossa Valley in South Australia where the climate is hot and dry.

**Below** The much cooler vineyards at high altitude in Trentino, northern Italy.

**Above** Huge stones in the vineyards of Châteauneuf-du-Pape retain the sun's heat.

**Below** The distinctive red soil of Coonawarra, Australia, helps give its red wines their elegant character.

# soil and terroir

Another critical factor in determining the character of wine is the soil of the vineyard. Yes, the very dirt where the vines grow affects the flavour. In Part Two of this book, you'll find many references to particular soil types and the character they bestow on individual wines, but here are one or two examples up front. Some limestone-rich areas, such as Chablis in France and Robertson in South Africa, are said to produce particularly good Chardonnay. The flint in Pouilly-sur-Loire's French soil is supposed to give the area's Sauvignon Blanc a smoky flavour. The free-draining red earth of Coonawarra in Australia yields excellent Cabernet Sauvignon. The large round stones in the vineyards of Châteauneuf-du-Pape retain the daytime heat and help produce ultra-ripe red grapes for powerful wine.

More generally, producers who care about quality look for difficult, stony, well-drained soils that force the vines to work hard. Viniculture is unlike horticulture; the aim is not to give the plants an easy ride with rich, soft, fertile soils, but to limit vigour and keep fruit yields relatively small. The objective is to produce tiny crops of grapes that contain lots of flavour, acidity, sugar and possibly tannin, but not water. To achieve this, the vines are kept somewhat stressed. Stony, free-draining soils make a vine work harder to find water, so it produces only a small, high-quality crop. Lots of vines are grown on well-watered, fertile plains for large harvests of cheap grapes, but this fruit tends to lack character and is almost always used for boring, basic wine.

The effect of a vineyard's site and soil on the character of wine is currently a hot topic. Winemakers talk about terroir, a quasi-mystical French concept that refers to a wine's origin, or the highly specific place where the grapes were grown. Terroir doesn't just mean the specific soil and climate, but also the gradient of the vineyard, its rainfall levels or the irrigation used instead, its proximity to the coast and other crops or wild plants growing nearby – in other words, just about anything affecting that particular plot of land.

Arguments over whether winemakers, grape varieties or terroir play the most important role in determining wine styles rage on. Until recently, it was clear that non-European winemakers thought they ruled the style; they believed they could turn out a palatable wine whatever the plot of land, while European producers, especially the French and Germans, believed that terroir was primarily responsible for a particular flavour or aroma. Now the two sides have become more closely aligned. Australians and Californians are beginning to place more emphasis on the fruit of individual regions or vineyards, and the French and Germans are realising that a winemaker can dictate a style to an extent by the methods employed in the winery. So now you know why the French put place-names on their wine labels, rather than grape varieties. They really do believe their wines reflect the character and personality of an area of land, and top producers try hard to express the character of a specific plot in the finished wine.

Rainfall is important, as we will see on page 20, but whether the water is retained in the soil is another factor to take into account. Well-drained soils are desirable, as the vine has to work to get down into the ground and reach the water. Many believe that means it picks up more interesting minerals along the way, which adds character to the wine. Soggy, water-logged soil is not good news, as all gardeners know full well. And neither is soil which has been stripped of all its natural nutrients – over-worked soil which has too much herbicide and artificial fertiliser in it, and which has been robbed of its essential character. It makes sense that this sort of soil wil not produce wine that reflects the natural terroir – hence the rise of organic viticulture (see page 13).

# major wine-producing regions of the world

The countries highlighted in the maps below are the important wine-producing regions of the world, the ones whose bottles you are most likely to come across at home. Grapes are grown for winemaking in numerous nooks and crannies across the globe, but only certain countries produce significant amounts of wine. Some are far more important than others, but a few are 'up-and-coming'. Look out for more bottles from these countries in the near future.

### Europe

France, Germany, Austria, Bulgaria, England (not UK), Greece, Hungary, Italy, Moldova, Romania, Slovakia, Slovenia, Spain, Switzerland, Portugal.

### Rest of the world

Argentina, Australia, Canada, Chile, India, Israel, Lebanon, Mexico, Morocco, New Zealand, South Africa (Western Cape only), USA, Uruguay.

# old vines and new vines

Vines produce grapes for a very long time; vineyards over one hundred years old are common in certain parts of the winemaking world. Such vines are highly prized for their small crops of concentrated grapes, which produce lots of intense flavour. You may think that young vines would produce livelier, fresher-tasting fruit, but they don't. Immature vines do not make particularly good wine, so winemakers usually wait several years for the plants to grow before making their finest bottles from this fruit. In the meantime, however, winemakers may make a second cheaper label from the grapes of newly planted vineyards.

Wines made from older vines sometimes say so on the label; look for the words *vieilles vignes* on French bottles. This is not a cast-iron guarantee of high quality, but it should (and usually does) indicate a richer, more concentrated style of wine. Older vineyards in parts of the southern hemisphere, which have churned out fruit for decades, are now being cherished for their small harvests of rich grapes. Old Shiraz vines in the Barossa Valley, Australia, are a fine example; used merely as 'workhorse' vines for over a century to create rough reds and fortified wines, they are now appreciated as producing first-rate fruit and are tended lovingly by top winemakers. They are quite a sight: their gnarled, twisted, grey forms like huge elephant trunks.

Crops can also be controlled by starving vines of water. In areas of low rainfall, irrigation is essential, but it must be carefully controlled to produce premium grapes. Irrigation is usually by a slow drip-feed, designed to keep the vines a little stressed but not so thirsty that they suffer badly. Note that some of the best winemaking regions in the world have low rainfall and no irrigation. Some of the traditional bush vines untrellised, round bushes grown close to the ground to retain water – are now regarded as excellent vines, because without irrigation they produce small crops of high-quality grapes.

Most vines are trained up onto a wire structure so that air flows freely through the shoots and the sun reaches any bunches of grapes. In damp areas, such as Galicia in northwest Spain, vines are raised high on pergolas to keep them away from the wet ground and reduce rot.

The exact clone of a vine is increasingly important as it affects the way your wine tastes. There are many clones of each variety, and in the case of a tricky vine like Pinot Noir, a clone can be selected to suit a specific climate or soil or to produce the flavours the winemaker wants. Often several clones are grown and blended. None of this has anything to do with genetic modification or hybrids (crosses of different vines). Clones are simply different strains of the same vine cultivated in nurseries.

**Above** A very new extensive planting of vines by the Yalumba company in South Australia.
**Below** By contrast, the vines in Henschke's Hill of Grace vineyard, Eden Valley, Australia, are over a century old.

# winemakers and their techniques

Now let's turn our attention to the people who make wine and the influence they can bring to bear on the liquid in your glass. Winemakers clearly make some major decisions, such as which grape varieties to use, where the fruit is sourced – although they don't always use their own grapes, but buy in their fruit from a specialist grower – and which techniques to use in the winery. In venerable winemaking areas of the world, these decisions are usually dictated by climate and tradition. A Rhône winemaker will probably work with Syrah and Grenache, say, making rich, concentrated wines with plenty of oak-ageing, while a German winemaker will most likely produce elegant Rieslings with no oak influence. And a winemaker in Beaujolais will usually use the carbonic maceration technique typical of this region, where the grapes are not crushed, but left in whole bunches fermenting slowly to produce low-tannin, fruity wines. But there are always mavericks, even in areas with a long history of winemaking.

The producers of a modern breed of wines, dubbed the 'Super-Tuscans', in central Italy are a case in point. They deliberately introduced international grapes into the local mix and to make premium reds outside the normal regulations for the region, and with cult success. Certain wineries in Rioja have long used Cabernet Sauvignon in the blend or substituted French oak for the traditional American barrels used in the region. Don't expect all winemakers to behave in the same way, even in the classic regions. Nowadays, anything goes.

Take the phenomenon of 'flying winemakers', who work in several regions of the world throughout the year. Some critics are appalled by this, believing that flying winemakers lead to uniform, 'identikit' wines across the world with a lack of regional flavour. My view is that flying-winemaker wines tend to be reliable, drinkable and generally of a higher standard than many cheapies from up-and-coming areas, but, on the whole, they don't tend to make the most exciting, characterful wines.

On a brighter note, the standard of everyday wine has improved a great deal over the past forty years or so. This is due, in part, to extra care over hygiene; wineries are cleaner places, some scrubbed and washed down regularly, rather like a hospital, and fewer grubby, spoiled wines are the result. Instead of concrete and fibreglass, stainless-steel containers are extensively used for fermenting wine; these gleaming metal vats are easier to keep clean. Grapes are brought in swiftly to the winery and crushed quickly, so they have less time to oxidise and lose their fresh aromas and flavours. Likewise, grapes are kept and fermented at controlled cool temperatures for the same reasons. All this helps the wine remain fresh and aromatic.

High-tech equipment is now commonplace in the winery – extra-gentle presses for squeezing the grapes without producing harsh tannins, electronic 'feet' for simulating the pounding of human soles on grape pulp, and machines that slowly turn bottles of sparkling wine upside down in an imitation of the 'riddling' technique found in Champagne (see pages 134–35). Some advances, including the last two mentioned, are clearly meant to save money, to make wine production a less labour-intensive and costly business. Other technologies are supposed to improve the quality of the wine, or at least, lead to more consistent results. A few of these innovations sound positively wacky. I have visited a winery where the sparkling wine was made in pyramids that were supposed to aid maturation. (It was a Feng Shui, energy-flow thing.) The wines were very good, I must admit, so maybe they were on to something, although it didn't make a lot of scientific sense.

Winemakers mess around with their wines more than you might imagine. They play with sugar and acidity levels (although the rules surrounding these practices are tighter in some countries than in others). Acidity tampering sounds unpleasant, but in fact, it involves the use of tartaric, citric or ascorbic powder to correct wines with naturally low acid levels, usually those from warm climates where the grapes get very ripe. Still sounds horrid? Well, these acids are naturally present in grapes anyway.

Here's something else that may come as a surprise: winemakers can also choose how to clarify the wine at the end of the fermentation process to remove any sediment or impurities. This is often done with egg white, or casein (a milk product), gelatin, even isinglass from fish bladders to which any particles cling before filtration. Vegetarians and vegans may want to look out for wines that have been clarified with bentonite clay only or are unfiltered. Some purists argue unfiltered reds taste more complex and interesting anyway. A few – but by no means enough – back labels are helpful in identifying the way in which wines have been treated.

Oak is the most obvious tool of the winemaker. The idea is that if wine is aged (and sometimes fermented *and* aged) in oak barrels it picks up some of the flavour of the wood, adding extra body and complexity to the finished wine. The amount of oak influence depends on how long it remains in barrel, how charred the inside of the barrels are, where the oak comes from, and even who the cooper was. Heavily charred or 'toasted' barrels give a richer, spicier flavour than lightly toasted ones, for example, while American oak has a creamier, more overtly vanilla flavour than French oak. The oak should always be well-balanced, enhancing the wine rather than overpowering it. The late twentieth century witnessed a lot of over-oaked wines, especially in the case of Chardonnay from the southern hemisphere. Thankfully, oak is being handled more carefully nowadays, with most winemakers treating it as a light seasoning rather than a crude addition. Oak chips are sometimes used instead of barrels; these are dunked in the wine, rather like tea leaves, to infuse the liquid with wood nuances. The result can be passable, but barrels tend to leave a subtler and more refined oak character.

## Flying winemakers

Flying winemakers, who first rose to prominence in the eighties and nineties, are much in evidence in areas of the winemaking world where the industry is still being developed – regions where there is a lot of potential, but few experienced producers with a good knowledge of the export market.

These winemakers fly in and out of each area, issuing orders and dictating the style of wine to be made to their minions, acting as long-distance consultants when they are not physically there. They will be in the northern hemisphere for the harvest, then set off for the same event in the southern hemisphere six months later. Flying winemakers are behind a number of widely available wines from southern France, South America, Eastern Europe, and Spain and Portugal, in particular.

Many flying winemakers are Australians, New Zealanders or Brits (who have usually trained in the Antipodes), who tend to argue that a decent wine can be crafted in most places on the earth, as long as the right techniques are applied.

# how to taste wine

Don't skip this if you assume tasting wine like a pro means looking like an idiot! Okay, it might do, but taking your time to think about this precious liquid will definitely help you learn an enormous amount about it. I reckon ninety-nine percent of all wine slips down our throats without touching the sides, so that while a little of its unique character comes through, not much does. If you look at wine carefully, then smell it properly, and finally take your time over tasting it, you should notice a lot of interesting characteristics starting to emerge,

### Look
The appearance of any wine can tell you much about the sort of style to expect.

### Sniff
Swirl the liquid to release its aroma – it's an important part of a wine's appeal.

for good or bad. Then you will almost certainly enjoy fine wine a great deal more. The best thing about tasting is that it's up to you what you think of a wine – no one is 'right' or 'wrong' in deciding what a wine tastes like. It's just a matter of building up points of reference that mean something to the individual taster. If you still think you'll look like an idiot, practise the following steps in the bath, spitting out at your toes – that's what a lot of the experts do – until it feels like second nature!

## Slurp

Swoosh the wine around your mouth to bring out the full flavour. Think about its taste and texture.

## Spit

The 'finish' of a wine is important. Consider its richness or lightness, length of flavour and general appeal.

## Look

The appearance of wine is important, so really peer at the liquid in your wine glass. It helps if you choose a plain glass, not a cut or coloured one, with a tall stem. Tipping the glass to one side helps, holding it way down the stem, especially when assessing the depth of colour in your red: look at the rim of the liquid, not the middle. A wine should look clear, not cloudy, without any bits of sediment floating in it. (Decant some reds and ports to avoid this, see pages 174–75). Look at the viscosity or otherwise of the liquid: a rich, thick wine leaves noticeable trails, or 'legs', down the side of the glass after you have swirled. This can indicate high alcohol levels or sweetness. Red wines with a purple, almost bluish tinge tend to taste younger than those with a brick-red, brownish colour, and those that have turned brown may well be past it. In whites, a deep-golden colour indicates a rich wine, which could well be oaky or lusciously sweet. A pale-straw hue means you have a drier, lighter style in your glass.

## Sniff

Now for the aroma. ('Bouquet' is another, somewhat old-fashioned term for describing the aroma of a wine; some experts call it the 'nose'.) Swirl the wine around your glass before smelling it, as this releases its aroma effectively. Now stick your nose near the liquid and take a big sniff, or a series of small sniffs. The scent of a wine is very important, acting as a crucial introduction to the flavour. This simple test is often overlooked, so linger over it. Does the wine smell appealing or not? Does it smell clean and fresh or sulphurous, vegetal or musty? Is it a subtle smell or a rich, pungent one? Think about the sort of fruit character in the aroma – citrus fruits, perhaps, or red berries, or bananas. You might take it further: what sort of citrus fruits (lemons, oranges, grapefruit...), what sort of red berries (raspberries, redcurrants...), are they fresh bananas or banana sweeties, or even banoffee pie? Look out for vanilla, cream, spice and pepper, too, as well as other more eclectic nuances.

## Slurp

Take a small sip and, instead of swallowing, swirl the liquid around your mouth, even drawing some air through it once you've sipped it and swooshing it around to release the full flavour. Look for similar characteristics in the flavour – fruit, cream, spice – but at the same time consider other elements in the taste of the wine, such as its the weight, body or structure and how acidic or refreshing it is. Try to decide whether this is a rich wine or a light one, a tart wine, or a heavy, dense or oily one. Is it tannic – tannins produce a furry sensation in the mouth, like sucking on a tea bag – or bone-dry or honeyed and sweet? Do you like this wine or not? Think about whether it is simply a big, rich, impressive wine, perhaps one that you might not want to drink in any quantity, but which is simply a show-off in character! Lighter, simpler wines can sometimes be more enjoyable or food-friendly. Finally, is the wine well-balanced, or does it have, for example, over-the-top tannins, mouth-puckering acidity or is its sweetness out of kilter?

## Spit

Professional wine tasters (almost) always spit wine out to save their sobriety, but they don't stop assessing the wine as they spit. The 'finish' of a wine is the final important factor. After you've spat the liquid out or swallowed it, does it leave a lingering flavour in your mouth or does it disappear from the taste buds in a disappointing way? This provides another opportunity to assess texture: is it a rich, gloopy wine or a thin, light one? Again, look out for those unusual nuances – perhaps ground pepper in a Syrah, ginger in a Gewürztraminer or chocolate in a Merlot – as these often come through on the finish more than ever. Sometimes wine faults show up on the finish. A corked wine might leave a musty taste in the mouth, while an over-acidic wine may be wincingly tart at the very end. Tannins also tend to show through at this stage more than any other. If your wine leaves a chewy, furry, 'tea-leaf' texture in your mouth, it's tannic and may need time to soften up, or a rare steak to accompany it.

## aromas and flavours

Wine doesn't only taste of grapes... In fact, the Muscat vine produces wine with 'grapes' as a classic tasting note, but that's about it. Wine more often seems to smell and taste of other fruits, as you have probably noticed, and sometimes tasters spot more unusual aromas and flavours. Chocolate, vanilla, pepper, honey and grass are just a few of the associations often noted in wine. Throughout Part Two of this book I have illustrated some of these common descriptors. Look out for these specific characteristics in the wines of each section – and be open to finding a few more of your own!

## tasting blind

Why not taste your wine 'blind', as professional judges do at competitions? This simply means the label is covered up – just use a brown paper bag or wrap foil round the bottle. Obviously it helps to have a guest if the wines are going to be a mystery for one person or the other. Take it further and invite a gang of friends round, get each to bring a wrapped-up bottle and do some blind wine tasting together.

# packaging

The vast majority of wines sold come in 75cl glass bottles. This standard size of bottle is supposed to be perfect for sharing between two, and anyway, if you don't finish it in one sitting, the wine should keep well for a couple of days. That said, I think there are alternatives that could be considered from time to time.

Half-bottles are a grand idea if you only want a glass or two; I recommend buying these rather than resealing a bigger bottle as wine does start to deteriorate from the moment it is exposed to air. Pick half-bottles if you are trying out new styles of wine, too, that way it won't matter so much if you choose something you don't like. Always buy halves for the sorts of wines that tend to be enjoyed at just one particular time of year, but are rejected the rest of the time. So, rather than bringing out the same dusty bottle of sherry each Christmas, buy a fresh half-bottle every year and finish it! I promise you, even fortified wines like sherry and port taste better when you crack open a new one. Any wine retailers worth their salt will stock a good range of halves. Make more of these small bottles.

Sadly, big bottles are equally over-looked. Why don't we buy more magnums (one and a half litres, the equivalent of two ordinary bottles) or even jereboams (six bottles)? Larger bottles look great at special celebrations, somehow convincing guests that we have been wildly generous when, in fact, an equal volume of wine bought in ordinary bottles usually costs about the same. Magnums are widely available for premium wine as well as for cheapies like Lambrusco and Liebfraumilch, although an independent wine merchant may be your best bet for tracking down a wide range of serious big bottles. Jereboams are rarer, and the huge Methuselahs (six litres, or eight bottles), Balthazars (sixteen bottles) and Nebuchadnezzars (twenty bottles) are even scarcer, and mainly restricted to Champagne.

If you want to buy large-format bottles for laying down in a cellar, bear in mind that the wine tends to age more slowly in them (and conversely more quickly in halves) – it's to do with the proportion of wine exposed to the sides and top of the bottle. Oh, and they won't fit in your normal wine racks, either!

Bottled wine is sealed with a natural cork, a plastic stopper or a screw cap. The characteristics of cork taint are discussed later in more detail (see page 178), but suffice to say here that an unacceptably high number of bottles are spoilt by the pesky mould that can occur when bark is used to plug a bottle. Metal screw caps are slowly coming into vogue and are being used by more quality wine producers than ever before. Although they seem less classy than natural cork, they fulfil their role of sealing wine well and bring no taint into the equation. Plastic stoppers have similar benefits. Plastic and metal screw caps are, however, not biodegradable and there is some debate over whether they allow wine to age well as they let no air in at all. Despite this, until cork manufacturers sort out their problems, it's my guess wine drinkers will increasingly seek out these alternative 'closures'. After all, you wouldn't buy milk in cartons if one in every twenty pints was spoilt by its packaging, would you? So why put up with cork taint?

Finally, wine boxes are a convenient container for wine if you are throwing a party and don't feel like opening bottles all night. Generally, they hold three litres of wine. Don't expect serious, sophisticated wine to come in boxes, as more everyday, easy-drinking styles tend to be packaged this way. I don't recommend boxes if you plan to siphon off just one glass from time to time, as the wine will deteriorate gradually in this type of packaging – or quickly, if a hole or leak develops in the bag, which sometimes happens. Use boxes for entertaining a crowd, and bear in mind some people think they look a bit naff!

# reading labels

It may be hard to imagine now, but just a few years ago the arrival of straightforward, clear wine labels was a revelation. Let's be honest, a lot of traditional wine labels are difficult to understand, referring as they do to obscure place-names, vineyard sites and different types of producers, such as *domaines*, *châteaux* and *négociants*. Highly parochial references to styles of wine – for example, *Spätlese* for a

### Classic French label
Grape varieties are not mentioned on traditional Bordeaux labels; the name of the château takes precedence.

### Traditional German label
In Germany, the grape variety does appear on the label – in this case, Riesling. Gothic script is common too; it looks old-fashioned, but don't let it put you off these often-great whites.

riper, and *Trocken* for a drier style of German white – make it even trickier to understand what is in the bottle. Thank goodness, then, for the younger winemaking countries which have pioneered labels giving exactly the information ordinary people wants to know. The wine is called, let's say, Muddy Creek, the grape is Chardonnay, the year was 1996 and the area was the Hunter Valley, Australia. Hallelujah!

## Modern, graphic labels

A typical label from a newer wine-producing country is simpler and easier to read. There is less clutter on the label – just a few words telling you the brand, the grape, the vintage and the region. And that's it. Easy!

## Classic sweet wine label

European dessert wines don't look much different to their dry counterparts. Look for areas that produce sweet styles.

## styles of wine labels

Newer wine-producing countries, like Australia and Chile, wines tend towards the same sort of labels: simple and obvious. But the lines are now blurred. Some European producers have followed suit and are turning out highly modern, graphic designs. The south of France and Germany are two places where a lot of modern-style labels are now being produced, particularly for cheapish wines that appeal to the everyday drinker.

As a general rule of thumb, though, the great classic wines of the world, such as Bordeaux, burgundy and German Rieslings, are still packaged under somewhat arcane labels that wine buffs understand, but everyone else finds a bit mystifying. I'm not suggesting that all wine should be labelled like an Aussie Chardonnay – we would lose the charming and culturally important traditional terminology of wine. I'm just pointing out that it isn't easy for beginners to understand wine labels. This is one of the reasons Europe has lost ground to the newer wine-producing regions in recent years.

## key words on wine labels

Throughout Part Two of this book, there are additional tips on terms found on a wine label from various regions, but here are some of the important elements to look out for:

• French wines are often labelled by place rather than grape variety. Don't expect to see 'Pinot Noir' on a bottle of red burgundy, or 'Cabernet and Merlot' on a bottle of red Bordeaux. The origin of the wine – in Bordeaux the château name, in Burgundy the place where the vines grew – will appear instead. You are meant to know the classic grapes of each region. Ditto the Loire and Rhône. In these areas, the place-names and producers appear on the label, but not Chenin Blanc, Syrah and so on.

• Alsace is an exception to this general rule. Winemakers in this region of eastern France do put grape varieties on the label. Otherwise Alsatian labels can be hard to get to grips with; they look German, sometimes with Germanic names and grapes, such as Riesling, and even use Gothic script on the label. Be aware that tall, green bottles are not always German; they may be from Alsace, or indeed from Austria or elsewhere.

• The south of France has recently adopted a simpler and more modern approach to labelling, imitating the newer wine regions and naming grape varieties. The wines often taste rather 'New World' in style, too: ripe, fruit-driven and very modern.

• Italian wines are generally not labelled by grape variety either – or rather, the great classics of Tuscany and Piedmont aren't. Modern producers working in the deep south and some of those in the northeast favour grapes appearing on labels.

• In Spain, the term 'oak-ageing' is particularly important, not only in Rioja but in other regions, too. Look out for terms such as *crianza* and *reserva* to indicate barrel maturation. The section on 'Full-bodied Reds' (see pages 104–119) has more details on this.

• Sparkling wines and Champagnes have a language of their own. *Brut* means 'dry' the world over. It is important to look for this word on a label if you want to avoid sugary froth. The term *méthode traditionnelle* is worth spotting, too, as it indicates the best method of making fizz, now adopted in various regions which make quality bubbly (see pages 130–143).

Somewhere on all bottles there will be the following information: the alcohol level (which can vary a great deal), the volume of liquid in the bottle (usually 75cl), the country of origin and the producer. It's likely that some phrase will indicate oak-ageing, if this took place, and the back label may tell you more about the region, the blend of grapes and the winemaker's aims. Other back labels will simply give you a load of hot air about the romantic peaks of the Chilean Andes or the sun-soaked vineyards of the warm Barossa Valley!

# tips for buying wine

Even those who have a good knowledge of wine can find it pretty disarming to be faced with rows and rows of bottles in a supermarket or off-licence. It's clearly easier to grab a familiar bottle every time, but as I have made clear throughout this book, that can mean you get stuck in a boring rut, always drinking the same grapes from the same region and even the same producer. The world of wine is so richly endowed with different styles that it would be a shame to get fed up with the liquid in your glass.

So the first and most essential tip to the wine shopper is be prepared to experiment. Make a point of avoiding a bottle that is tried and tested in your house; instead plump for something quite different, be it a new grape variety – how about Viognier, Sémillon, Cabernet Franc? – or a new region: Argentina, Portugal and Greece are all fascinating right now. In particular, avoid the very big brands. There may be nothing wrong with them, and they may well represent reasonable quality, reliable wine at a decent price, but everyone drinks them and they usually fail to offer much excitement. With smaller producers you are more likely to get a handcrafted, characterful product. And besides, your neighbours won't all have it in their wine racks too!

Think about the various outlets that offer wine and decide which ones work best for you on different occasions. Supermarket wine departments have been revolutionised since the late twentieth century and these outlets stock an impressive range of styles and price points. Their turnover is fast, so wines are likely to be fresh, and they can offer worthwhile discounts because of their buying power. Supermarkets are convenient, of course, as you can buy your booze at the same time as your weekly food shop and choose wines that match your cooking easily.

On the other hand, some argue that supermarkets still lack the knowledgeable assistance offered by a specialist merchant. A fine independent wine merchant is certainly a great place to go if you are searching for something different and might need help in choosing. Make sure you quiz the assistant hard and perhaps even ask for a taste of wine – independents sometimes have a bottle or two of interesting stuff open to try.

It's worth seeking out a specialist merchant if you are developing a love of a particular type of wine. Some specialise in Bordeaux, burgundy or German wines, for example, and now there are a few impressive smaller outlets with a serious emphasis on non-European wines. Don't forget mail order or internet wine buying, too; those who are housebound or who lack a car find these particularly useful. Always use a well-established, reputable company, however.

Look out for 'bin end' offers, which indicates the end of a stock of wine (a few bottles left over that are being sold at a special price). In general, though, be sure to avoid wines that are past it, looking tired and stewing gently on a dusty shelf (see also pages 48, 129 and 162).

Finally, take a good look at any information you are offered in-store: shelf descriptions or press recommendations (not a fool-proof guide to your own likes and dislikes, but probably a fair indication of the style of wine), labels, leaflets and in-store magazines. We all need as much help as possible when buying wine if we can't actually taste the stuff, so make good use of what is there to help in your decision.

# 2 the styles

# light, dry whites

Their detractors write off the light, dry whites as boring and flavourless, but those in the know point to some of these wines as the most elegant and refreshing around. A few are even complex and satisfying, providing you know where to look. It's unfortunately true that along the way you will encounter some flavourless, mediocre bottles. A premium light, dry white has a lovely crispness, some tantalising, subtle fruit flavours and, perhaps, a pretty, aromatic hint of blossom. It may be delicate, but a good light white wakes up the palate, makes the mouth water and whets the appetite like no other table wine. It also washes down a range of summery dishes wonderfully well – leafy salads, tomatoes and basil, white fish and pasta in creamy sauces. And it leaves you wanting more: the greatest quality of a fine, light white is how easygoing and enjoyable it is – unlike, say, a heavily oaked Chardonnay that may effortlessly win a wine competition, but which you don't want to drink in any great quantity. Light, dry whites should always be highly drinkable and moreish.

So, how to avoid those dull bottles and find the right one? Cool climates count for a lot; pick a wine from a place where the grapes retain pure fruit flavours and that essential 'zing' of acidity. Warm climates just don't do the same trick. Go for the better grape varieties – Riesling, Verdicchio and Grüner Veltliner – which are more likely to make wine with flavour, rather than second-rate ones – Müller-Thurgau and Trebbiano – which generally produce uninspiring, bland whites. Riesling, in particular, is in a league of its own. With all light, dry whites, if you can track down a winemaker who uses low-yielding vines (for more concentration in the grapes) rather than fertile, high-cropping ones, that's all to the good. Not much on the label will tell you this, but some of the tips on the next few pages will point you towards the right wines. Trading up a notch from the basic, rustic whites, churned out as cheap-and-cheerful gluggers, will help you avoid the sort of wine that's a yawn and instead give you a crisp, zesty wake-up call to the senses!

**APPEARANCE** Pale-straw colour, sometimes with light-green hints. Not golden-yellow like richer or sweeter white wines.

**TEXTURE** Relatively thin, light, watery, neither viscous nor weighty.

# light, dry whites

AROMA Good examples smell of fresh, tangy citrus fruit: lemons, limes, grapefruit and crunchy green apples. Some have a floral note, others a hint of almond. Second-rate, dull examples have little aroma or smell grubby.

FLAVOUR Should have a refreshing, succulent streak of acidity. Again, look out for those citrus fruits and freshly chopped apples. A clean, crisp, mineral finish.

# Riesling

The Riesling grape is refreshing in more ways than one. Of course, as anyone who has tried true Riesling will know, it is one of the world's greatest aperitifs – naturally light and elegant yet racy, with mouth-watering citrus and apple fruit and a crisp finish. So it's refreshing in the most obvious sense of the word. But Riesling is also refreshing in that it makes a welcome change from all the Chardonnay and Sauvignon Blanc that fills our shop shelves. It is a quite different style of wine, as will become clear below. But why the need to say 'true' Riesling? That's because this poor grape gets blamed – unfairly – for a lot of the light, white dross out there. Many have the wrong idea about Riesling; they think it's the variety behind all the blandest, least memorable light whites, when in fact much cheaper, less well-known grapes are usually responsible for these. If I handed you a glass of fine Riesling, you'd probably be amazed at how much delicious flavour there is in it – and how delightfully fresh, tangy and vivacious the wine seems. So don't confuse Riesling with lesser wines. It's consistently delightful, and remarkably long-lived to boot. In fact, for many serious wine buffs, this is the greatest white grape of them all.

**GERMANY** Fine German Riesling is a very different creature from cheap and nasty German plonk, so if you've never tried it, give it a go. It's no surprise that this type of wine is often described as one of the trade's best kept secrets – there are plenty of aficionados out there loving it despite its untrendy image! The cool climate here produces wines that are never over-the-top – restraint, subtlety and elegance are the watchwords here. Alcohol levels remain naturally low – seven or eight percent is not unusual in a German Riesling, and nine or ten percent is quite common (compared to twelve to fourteen percent in other table wines).

That said, the style does vary from bottle to bottle – too much so sometimes, as it can be hard to know exactly what type of Riesling you are getting by looking at the label. Here are some tips: the Mosel region makes the prettiest, most delicate examples, with a spring-like, apple-blossom scent, although there is still a spine-tingling acidity in many; the Rheingau makes steelier, more intense, fuller-bodied versions, while the Pfalz is a progressive region that is moving with the times and turning out slightly more juicy, fruity, modern styles.

The main problem is to pick a level of sweetness that you enjoy – whether it's bone-dry and bracing, medium with a dab of honeyed weight or luscious and sticky.

Germany makes Riesling with all levels of sweetness, but you may not find reading those densely written Gothic labels very easy. This, incidentally, is one reason fine German wines have gone out of fashion – consumers find the words on, say, an Australian bottle of wine much easier to follow.

For the record: the word *trocken* on a label means dry, while *halbtrocken* means semi-dry. Meanwhile, the top quality category of Riesling (these bottles say *Qualitätswein mit Prädikat* or QmP on the label), ones made to certain strict rules and regulations, are divided into six categories according to the ripeness of the grapes used, and this (rather roughly) corresponds to their dryness/sweetness levels. *Kabinett* indicates dry, *Spätlese* is a riper, often off-dry style, and *Auslese*, *Beerenauslese*, *Trockenbeerenauslese* and *Eiswein* follow next in order of increasing sweetness. (For more on this, go to the section on 'Sweet Wines', see pages 144–155.) Then there are certain wines which have been made from fruit grown in the best sites – *Erstes Gewächs*, or 'first growth'. These specific vineyard areas are named on the label.

Complicated? Yes. German Riesling takes a bit of getting to know. But it's worth it. Once you have convinced yourself, try these tantalising, lip-smacking whites on your friends; if they are dubious, then let them taste it before telling them it's a German wine. I bet most of them love it and are converted to the joys of Riesling.

On the other hand, there are some small signs now that German Riesling is set to become a bit more fashionable. Most people have got over their obsession with chunky, oaky southern hemisphere whites and recognise that there are other, more subtle, white wines out there. The prices are fair – very fair, in fact – and a good Riesling is wonderfully food-friendly in a way that a monster Californian Chardonnay will never be. Finally, don't miss the chance to try an older German Riesling. If stored correctly, it will lose its spiky, acid edge, softening and mellowing and taking on a more honeyed, toffee-apple appeal. Then there's something else about older Riesling – it acquires a distinct whiff of lanolin and petrol. That sounds horrible, but it isn't; instead, it gives a lovely warm, mellow richness to the older wines. Give them a go – you have to try aged Riesling for yourself to see what I mean. Once you've started drinking German Riesling, you can become an expert by comparing wines from particular vineyard sites, as they give a fascinating insight into the effects of different soils and micro-climates. Recommended producers include: Müller-Catoir, Dr. Loosen, Bürklin-Wolf, Lingenfelder, J.J. Prüm.

## Making the difference

Light, dry whites have improved no end in quality over the past fifteen years or so; put simply, they are more reliably fresh, clean and crisp than they used to be. This is due partly to more sensitive handling of the grapes between picking and fermenting, so that subtle flavours are not lost, and partly to the use of low, controlled temperatures during fermentation. The wine is fermented in stainless-steel tanks – much more hygenic than concrete vats. Indeed, hygiene is considered very important at wineries these days, and light, dry whites have benefitted hugely. There are still some oxidised, faded or plain grubby whites around, but fewer now than ever before.

## Matching light, dry whites with food

Successful food-and-wine matching is all about balancing like with like or, in this case, light with light. Never match a tart, lean, dry white with very rich food or any form of red meat. However, these wines go well with crisp dishes such as tomato salad, grilled peppers and asparagus, and even stand up reasonably well to fruity or acidic salad dressings. They are great with white fish dishes, simple fresh seafood and, more surprisingly, they are good at washing down mild chicken and vegetable curries. Sauvignon Blanc is a wow with goat's cheese.

**FRANCE** The second-best place in the world for Riesling is Alsace in eastern France. This region is on the French border with Germany and has at several times during its history been part of Germany, so it's hardly surprising that Riesling is an important grape here. Wines from Alsace even look confusingly Germanic, with a tall bottle shape, Germanic names and sometimes Gothic script on the label, so be careful to distinguish the two – they are quite different in taste. Alsace Rieslings have a richer, more full-bodied character, and the alcohol levels are usually higher – back up to normal table-wine levels rather than unusually low. They should still have that tell-tale streak of fresh acidity, though, and the best examples should age well.

Look out for the *grand cru* wines – over fifty of the best vineyard sites (*grands crus*, named on the label) are meant to indicate the best fruit in the region. Some are superb, but others don't quite deserve the honour and extra cost that a *grand cru* wine can fetch. Match them with richer food than German Rieslings, such as fish in creamy sauces, or cheese-and-onion tarts. Good producers: Trimbach, Zind-Humbrecht and, for good value, Turckheim.

**REST OF EUROPE** Austria makes some impressive dry Riesling, with tart, intense lemon fruit and a bracing mineral quality. Some have a weighty, full texture (expect thirteen percent alcohol – much higher than in Germany) and should age well. Try one made near Vienna or from the region of Styria or, best of all, from the Wachau region in Lower Austria, where the decidedly cool climate and well-drained soils help create some brilliant wines. Bründlmayer, Hirtzberger, FX Pichler are names to look out for. A few rather lean, but refreshing Rieslings are made in northern Italy, mostly in the cool northeast of the country. Go for wines from the Trentino or Alto-Adige regions.

**REST OF THE WORLD** Australian Riesling is a 'must-try' – you will see a completely different side to the grape. Sure, the crisp acidity is still there, and that citrus fruit is to the fore, but this is a riper type of Riesling, a sun-kissed wine, with juicy lime the most obvious characteristic. Given enough time (five years or more), that crisp edge softens and toasty, honeyed layers start to appear, while that freshly chopped fruit becomes more like lime marmalade… Delicious! A hint of petrol or kerosene can be spotted in properly matured examples. Clare Valley and Eden Valley (both in the south) and Tasmania are key regions for Australian Riesling. Interestingly, before the boom in Chardonnay plantings, Riesling was the most widely planted white grape Down Under, and now winemakers seem to have revived their interest, so look out for a growing number on the shelves. Labels to try include Mount Langi Ghiran, Tim Adams and Henschke, and even the cheaper Jacob's Creek Dry Riesling is a corker!

While we're in the Antipodes, don't miss out on New Zealand Riesling. It's similar to the Australian style, bursting with citrus fruit, but has a pithier, more mineral-dry edge. The South Island wine regions make the best – especially Marlborough, Central Otago and Canterbury. Felton Road, Giesen, Villa Maria and Hunter's all produce fine examples.

Canada is another country excelling with dry Riesling – pity the wines are not more widely available. The sweet Rieslings of Canada are more renowned (see page 153) but if you come across a dry one, snap it up. In the United States, most wine is sourced from California, but not Riesling. Although a few decent West Coast examples do exist (from high-altitude, cool sites), better Riesling has come out of Washington State, Oregon and the Finger Lakes in New York State, where winemakers concentrated on this variety while the Californians went mad for Chardonnay.

# Sauvignon Blanc

Sauvignon Blanc can be very fruity and pungent, and because of this the grape is dealt with in more detail in the next section, 'Fruity, Spicy Whites' (see pages 50–61). Nonetheless, light, lean Sauvignons do exist in the form of Sancerre and Pouilly-Fumé and other wines from the cool Loire Valley.

**FRANCE**  Sancerre is perhaps the most famous appellation for Sauvignon Blanc – it can produce extremely attractive, bone-dry, lemony wines, while nearby Pouilly-Fumé wines are known for their mineral, slightly smoky note (think of a spark of gun-flint; the whiff of smoke from a fired pistol).

The best vineyards where these wines are produced have chalk over clay soils, with some patches of flint, the latter known as silex soils and said to produce the most long-lived wines. Top Sancerre and Pouilly-Fumé are, for many, the most elegant and hauntingly beautiful Sauvignons of all, and from a fine winemaker such as Cotat Frères, De Ladoucette or Didier Dagueneau, so they are, but many inferior wines exist, too, and prices are not low. Better-value premium Sauvignon sometimes comes from less well-known parts of the Loire – Quincy, Reuilly and Menetou-Salon, while for everyday quaffing, Sauvignon de Touraine and *Vin de Pays de la Jardin de la France* Sauvignon (Loire 'country wines' made from this grape) can hardly be bettered for simple, zesty refreshment at a very reasonable price.

Further southwest, around the wider Bordeaux area, plenty of simple quaffing wines made from Sauvignon alone or Sauvignon and Sémillon are produced. The great oaked Bordeaux whites have no place in this section as they are certainly not light, but basic Bordeaux Blanc and whites from Bergerac and Entre-Deux-Mers provide a vast sea of Sauvignon of variable quality. A superior example is lemony and dry with a distinct note of freshly chopped grass. Sauvignon in the guise of *Vin de Pays du Gard* is on specially good form at the moment. It would be wrong to generalise hugely about so much wine, but while most are palatable, south west Sauvignon doesn't generally have the snappy, pure Sauvignon character that the Loire provides.

**REST OF EUROPE**  Austria is the source of fine Sauvignon, bracingly crisp and mouth-watering, the best of which is made in the Styria region to the south. Some have startlingly high acidity, guaranteed to wake up tired taste buds, although toned-down, less nervy wines, even some rich, oak-aged ones, have started to emerge more recently. Northern Italy is another important destination for the Sauvignon lover, the cool, high-altitude vineyards of the Friuli-Venezia-Guilia and Trentino-Alto Adige regions making simple, lean, racy Sauvignons that are refreshing but no more complex than that.

## Storing and serving

Serve the light, dry whites nice and cold to emphasise their refreshing, mouth-watering tanginess. Store in the fridge for at least an hour or two before serving, then keep the bottle cool by putting it on ice or back in the fridge. Serve in medium-sized white wine glasses (nothing too small or you won't get the full benefits of those delicate aromas as you swirl the glass). A long-stemmed, elegant, plain glass is perfect for holding and seeing your wine. Very light, simple, dry whites need drinking up as soon as you buy them, as they will lose their fragile fragrance and fruit flavour quickly. Good, crisp Sauvignon should stand up better for a few months, while fine Riesling is surprisingly long-lived. Drink it up when young sometimes, but do try an older Riesling once in a while for a taste of honeyed apple, yet a dry finish, and even that famous hint of petrol on the aroma.

# Other light, dry whites

### Welschriesling/Laski Rizling

Don't make the mistake of thinking that all whites with Riesling/Rizling on the bottle are true Riesling. Welschriesling, aka Laski Rizling, has nothing to do with our fine German friend, and it makes much less exciting light, dry whites. These wines tend to be bland with lower acidity (i.e. less refreshing) and they certainly don't age well, turning flat and dull within a matter of months. A few palatable examples of Welschriesling come from Austria, but in general, this grape should be avoided in favour of real Riesling.

### Muscadet/Melon de Bourgogne

Taste a poor Muscadet and you wonder what all the fuss is about – it's simple, perhaps a little too tart, and frankly rather boring. Certainly nothing to write home about. The product of the area around Nantes in France's Loire Valley, this wine is a little overrated. Even the best examples fail to thrill. But there is a big jump in quality from basic Muscadet to the finest wines.

Premium Muscadet is aged on its yeast sediment (lees), which gives it a creamier edge, perhaps with a hint of fresh bread or even yoghurt, and in youth, a fresh prickle on the tongue of carbon dioxide gas. Quality is on the up in the Loire Valley; and there are better wines around than there were a decade ago. Look out for the words *sur lie* on a label indicating a wine that has been bottled on the lees. Avoid the bargain basement here.

Melon de Bourgogne, by the way, is the real name for the grape that makes Muscadet. Good Muscadet is a decent wine for washing down seafood, especially oysters.

### Müller-Thurgau

This is the main grape behind many cheap, once-popular German whites that are now less fashionable: Liebfraumilch, Niersteiner, Piesporter and Hock. There is nothing inherently wrong with a clean, fresh example, but don't expect much.

Müller-Thurgau has very little character compared with Riesling (which is, ironically, one of its parents – this is a modern cross between Riesling and a more obscure grape variety) and it has hardly any fragrance or complexity, but growers love it because the vine flourishes easily and produces loads of fruit.

Although plantings are in decline now, it is still widely planted in Germany and it's a similar story in New Zealand: Müller-Thurgau was a major player here until recently when other grapes proved more popular. Drinkers simply discovered wines with better flavours and it fell from grace. It is just about possible to make a half-decent Müller-Thurgau, and a few producers in Germany and New Zealand do so (as well as one or two in Italy and, believe it or not, England) but it takes a lot of care in the vineyard, and very low yields to make interesting wine.

### Pinot Grigio and other Italian whites

We're talking Pinot Grigio, Frascati, Soave and Orvieto here – a quartet of Italian whites that all taste light, clean, crisp and fresh. That's the idea, anyway. In reality there are too many oxidised and disappointing examples of all four around.

The mediocre, characterless Trebbiano grape plays a major part in the production of Frascati, Soave and Orvieto. Cheap examples use mainly Trebbiano, while better bottles use a higher proportion of a tastier grape such as Garganega in Soave.

Pinot Grigio is the same as France's Pinot Gris grape, which makes rich and opulent wines in Alsace, but light, lemony, sometimes spritzy whites in Italy. If you want to buy it, try to find bottles that are fresh into the shop rather than those which have been hanging around collecting dust, as Pinot Grigio doesn't last well. And go for a reputable producer – top Soave, say, from a fastidious winemaker, has bags more flavour than mass-produced, dirt-cheap Soave.

Frascati, Soave and Orvieto come from Lazio, Verona and Umbria, respectively. At their best, Frascati and Orvieto taste of fresh lemons with a hint of floral violet aroma. Soave can be more interesting, with creamier depths and a richer note of almond oil from a top producer (Pieropan is one name to look out for). Although these wines are more easily available, lesser-known whites from the central Marches region made from a grape called Verdicchio (this appears on the label) are more exciting: still fresh and snappy, but with a greater depth of limey flavour. If you enjoy light Italian whites, do give Verdicchio a whirl.

## Dry Muscat
The Muscat family of related grape varieties is a large and widespread one, and many of the wines produced by its scions are sweet (see page 149). But aromatic, dry Muscat is well worth a taste if you come across it.

This is the only white wine that truly tastes of grapes above any other fruit – crunchy green grapes fresh from the fridge in the case of crisp, young, cold Muscat. As such it is a pretty, summery wine indeed – perfect for hot days sitting in the garden, should any come our way!

Dry Muscat is a speciality of Alsace in eastern France (try it with fresh asparagus) and there are a few great-value examples from Italy, Austria and Germany (where it is called Muskateller), and also Australia (try Brown Brother's), too.

## Ugni Blanc and Colombard
Colombard's roots are firmly in the Cognac region of France where it has been a mainstay of brandy production for centuries. One of the reasons it works so well in brandy is that the base wine it produces is neutral in character, so there you go – it makes pretty boring table wine.

In the right hands, though, it can be fairly crisp and quaffable and it does have a light, floral edge. It is blended with Ugni Blanc to make the snappy, refreshing country wine *Vin de Pays des Côtes de Gascogne* and is also used for basic but palatable light whites in South Africa. Ugni Blanc is called Trebbiano in Italy (where it plays a major role in the Italian whites described above). It does not have enough natural character to create interesting wine.

## Grüner Veltliner
Austria's very own white grape makes distinctive wines with a clear note of white pepper twisted over racy citrus fruit. Not yet well-known overseas, Grüner Veltliner can produce some strikingly good wines, wonderfully dry and lean yet full of flavour, and the best will even taste weighty and rich in texture, if tangy and succulent, and will age well for a couple of years. One to try if you fancy a change from the usual suspects! Bründlmayer and Freie Weingärtner Wachau (FWW) are labels to sample.

## Aligoté
Burgundy is famous for its world-beating Chardonnays (see also pages 66–67), but another white grape grows there, too. Aligoté is not nearly as important in the region as Chardonnay, nor does it create anything like such impressive wine, but as with many of the grapes described above, it can make a refreshing change. It generally produces wines that are tart and light, sometimes with a very slight spritz of gas, but a ripe example from a warm vintage can be a little creamier and fuller than this.

Traditionally, this is the base wine for 'kir' – add a splash of crème de cassis (from Dijon if you want to be loyal to Burgundy!) to a glass of young, cold Aligoté for a wonderful summer aperitif.

# shortcuts to success

## FIRST TASTE

• If a light, dry white isn't refreshing, then there's something seriously wrong with it! These wines are meant to be mouth-watering, palate-cleansing, tangy and crisp, so reject any examples that taste flat and flabby – in other words, lacking in zesty fruit and acidity. They may be corked or just badly made, but they won't reach the spot!

• Try to savour the delicate aromas and flavours of these wines. They are not the most extrovert characters in the wine world, but even the most committed fan of full-on, ultra-fruity Chardonnay can learn to love the elegance and subtlety of these very different wines as well, if they take time to stop and notice the more restrained but often complex layers of scent and taste here.

• If you are bored with dull, light whites, try wines made from premium grape varieties only and from top spots – Riesling from the Mosel in Germany, say, or Sauvignon Blanc from Sancerre in the Loire Valley. Avoid the cheapest wines from less interesting grapes.

• Be aware that some light whites are much drier than others. Some are medium and will taste distinctly sweet for those used to bracing, bone-dry whites. That doesn't necessarily mean they are poor quality, but they may not be to your taste. If you aren't sure what's in your bottle, try before you buy.

# BUYER'S GUIDE

• Unless you are buying mature Riesling, always aim to buy young, light whites. Bag the most recent vintage you can, and if the wine is non-vintage, try to check with the shop that it is a recent shipment. Never buy light whites that have been sitting around too long, especially if they look dusty or the liquid has turned darker yellow. They've almost certainly had it and will taste dull.

• Some inexpensive French wines in this style provide good value – young Vin de Pays des Côtes de Gascogne, or Sauvignon de Touraine, is heartwarmingly cheap, yet reliably fresh and appealing. Don't expect anything too exciting, though.

• Further up the quality ladder, Riesling can be remarkably cheap. This is partly because the grape has been out of fashion for a long time (except among wine aficionados, who have always loved it). Germany in particular offers some seriously good, light, white Riesling for little outlay. Snap up these gems before someone else does.

• Remember that the best light, dry whites – the crispest, tangiest, most tantalisingly subtle, light whites – come from cooler climates. Wines made in this style from hotter areas tend to taste bigger, riper and sometimes even oily – fine if you like that kind of thing, but not truly very 'light' and sometimes lacking finesse and subtlety.

# MOVING ON

• As Germany and Austria make some of the best light, dry whites, don't be put off by the old-fashioned Gothic script and seemingly difficult labels on their wines. The faint-hearted can always turn back to a boring big brand from Australia – be brave and give these hidden treasures a try!

• Once you've sampled fine German white wine, never buy the cheap and nasty bottles from the same country again. German wine is divided into the great and the gruesome – avoid the bland commercial cheapies.

• Venture further afield and try light, dry whites from unusual places like Hungary, Austria, northern Italy and Switzerland, not just from France and Germany.

• Never try to pair the light, dry whites with very rich food – they will be overpowered by roast turkey and all the trimmings, or spicy sausages and gravy – so stick to light partners with these wines or serve them alone as aperitifs – these wines are just fine on their own.

# fruity, spicy whites

If you don't like your whites too pallid and wishy-washy, but you hate oaky, powerful whites, then linger over the next few pages. It can sometimes seem hard to find those 'in-between' whites, as we all appear to be drowning in a sea of rich Chardonnay or weedy Liebfraumilch. Here, then, are the medium-bodied whites, many with ripe fruit and a heady perfume, but very few of them oaky. The wines that feature on these pages are either overtly fruity, packed with juicy, succulent flavour, like New Zealand Sauvignon Blanc, or they have a spicy hint, like Alsace Gewurztraminer. These wines have zoomed back into vogue of late, often replacing Chardonnay as a more refreshing type of white that still packs a punch. And as we shall see, these wines are amazingly food-friendly, matching the most trendy dishes around.

You won't be impressed by everything that falls into this category. All styles of wine bring the odd let-down, and in the case of these, it usually comes in the form of a disappointingly dilute bottle which fails to deliver a loud blast of character. Or it can be because the wine is too flabby; it lacks firm acidity to give a fresh streak to all that fruit and spice. Then there is the level of sweetness – often a tricky problem with white wine. A bone-dry glass is expected but instead you get something faintly sugary – or vice versa. The good news is that most modern producers make crisp, dry wines and in the case of Alsace, you can avoid the sweet wines (see also page 149). Then again the medium wines can be so wonderful that you may not even mind that honeyed tinge.

**TEXTURE** Medium – not exactly viscous, but not nearly as thin as the light whites.

**APPEARANCE** Straw-coloured, heading towards gold hints, sometimes a little green. Not as pale as the light whites, but less richly coloured than heavily oaked or many sweet wines.

# fruity, spicy whites

**AROMA** Terrific! Fruity whites have citrus or tropical fruits or apple leaping out of the glass. Grass, green pepper, even tomato leaves can be found, too. Sauvignon Blanc can be very pungent, with ripe gooseberry, asparagus and even a hint of tom-cat or sweat. Spicy whites have a heady, exotic perfume. A scent of roses is often found, along with cake spices (nutmeg, ginger), lychees… even Turkish delight.

**FLAVOUR** Lots of interesting nuances similar to those found on the scent, although good fresh fruit should be at the core. Should have a clean, crisp finish.

# Sauvignon Blanc

More and more of us are waking up to the joys of Sauvignon Blanc in all its different manifestations. A few years ago Chardonnay seemed to be everywhere and the only famous and popular style of Sauvignon Blanc was Sancerre. Now Sauvignon (you don't need to say 'blanc' all the time) has stepped out from Chardonnay's shadow and become a fashionable grape variety sourced from many different countries. It's well-loved partly because it offers a different, racier, leaner mouthful than Chardonnay, and partly because it is hardly ever barrel-aged, so it appeals to those who dislike oak. But be aware that there is a wide range of Sauvignon. Some of the most famous wines made from this variety, like the Sauvignons from the cool Loire Valley in France, are distinctly subtle and elegant, and as such, they are dealt with in the first section of our guide to wine styles (see page 44), along with the bracingly fresh and light Sauvignons of Austria and northern Italy. Although these wines have a certain clean, lemony quality, they could not be described as fruit-driven and ripe. Anyone who has tried a Sauvignon Blanc from the southern hemisphere, however, will know that these are more extrovert wines. Most warm-climate Sauvignons are richly aromatic and ultra-fruity, packed with bright, vivacious perfume and flavour. There are plenty of Sauvignons that hover between the reserved French and the louder New Zealand styles, but generally speaking, most New World examples fall firmly into the fruity category. And these are the wines that have woken up the modern world to Sauvignon Blanc and just what a refreshing thrill it can provide.

**NEW ZEALAND** New Zealand's wines weren't famous for anything much until Marlborough Sauvignon Blanc hit the scene. Back in the seventies, this was a winemaking country that turned out some reasonable whites but didn't get the critic's pulse racing. The beautiful, cool, Marlborough region in the South Island was mainly covered in fields and sheep, not vines. Then something remarkable happened. A couple of wineries thought it would be a good idea to plant the Sauvignon Blanc grape – best known for making dry whites in France's Loire Valley and Bordeaux – in the stony, well-drained soils of Marlborough's valleys. They reckoned that the low night-time temperatures there and the long, gradual ripening season, as well as that rocky terrain, might just produce decent white wine from this particular grape. And they were right.

It's still hard to believe that Marlborough Sauvignon only hit our shop shelves in the eighties. It seems like a style of wine that has always been there – a classic. Although it is still a newcomer (compared to Sancerre, Pouilly-Fumé and Bordeaux Sauvignon blends) that is

exactly what it has become: a modern classic, a new type of white wine made by planting a traditional French grape variety in a totally different part of the world. The Sauvignon from this little corner of a small island in the Antipodes took everyone by storm. From the first sniff of crunchy, fresh gooseberries to the underlying hints of tomato leaf, herbs, grass, tom-cat (yes, really, but it's not as bad as it sounds), asparagus and passion-fruit, New Zealand Sauvignon is utterly distinctive.

It's possible to get bored with that relentless, rather over-the-top, pungent gooseberry character, but most wine-lovers come back to New Zealand Sauvignon sooner or later for a reminder of just how vibrant and bright white wine can be. It's certainly a wonderful antidote to dull, insipid whites (of which far too many examples still exist). Ring the changes to some extent by trying examples from other parts of New Zealand. Although Marlborough remains the most important region for Sauvignon (many, many wineries now make it there and the sheep have had to find new pastures), there are other spots on both islands that do well with this grape, too. Still on the South Island, the regions of Nelson, near to Marlborough, Central Otago further south, and Canterbury, near the town of Christchurch, are important Sauvignon sources (expect a slightly leaner, crisper character from Canterbury), while on the North Island, Martinborough (or Wairarapa, as it is also known) is the source of some impressive, savoury and rich Sauvignon. Hawke's Bay on the North Island makes several good examples as well.

Don't stick to one winery, either, even if it is a fashionable label. There are plenty of quality wines to choose from, so taste around New Zealand Sauvignon a bit more. A few Sauvignons have a small amount of Semillon in the blend; others are made with a proportion aged for a short time in oak for a subtle roundness; others still are deliberately turned out lean, herbaceous and grassy. Of the myriad labels, Hunter's, Isabel Estate, Jackson Estate, Vavasour and Palliser are all well worth sampling, and the most famous New Zealand wine of all, the cultish Cloudy Bay Sauvignon Blanc, is still on fine form, though it can be horribly expensive to buy in restaurants. Some of the cheaper New Zealand Sauvignons offer better value for money, so try Montana, Villa Maria and even own-label supermarket wines like Sanctuary.

**SOUTH AFRICA** South Africa is going great guns with Sauvignon at the moment. Although the Cape's wine industry fell behind the rest of the world during the dark days of apartheid, there is now a new sense of excitement about South African wine, and Sauvignon is emerging as one of the most successful white grapes of the modern era. The style of modern Cape Sauvignon falls somewhere between the elegance of the Loire wines and the richer fruitiness of New Zealand – perfect for many drinkers who find one too restrained and the other too overtly pungent. Tasters may notice an attractive lime and passion-fruit streak and possibly a hint of green capsicum, rather than the gooseberry and tom-cat of New Zealand

## Making the difference

The best Sauvignon Blanc is grown in relatively cool-climate vineyards, so the grapes retain their crisp acidity and mouth-watering fruit flavours, rather than turning flabby and oily. But cool climates bring another potential problem: lack of ripeness, especially as Sauvignon is a vigorous vine which tends to send a vast green canopy over the grapes, shading them from the sun. One answer to this is canopy management, when the leaves are cut back to expose the grapes to sunlight and air. By using careful canopy management, growers can achieve sufficient ripeness in grapes without having to replant in warmer areas. In an area famous for Sauvignon, like Marlborough in New Zealand, the bright daytime sunshine and colder night-time temperatures bring about well-balanced grapes with intense fruit flavours as well as crisp acidity.

Sauvignon. Exciting wine is now being made in several parts of the Western Cape, including the Robertson and Constantia regions. Try Springfield, Klein Constantia or Vergelegen brands.

**CHILE**  Unfortunately, it's not always possible to know when you are getting true Sauvignon Blanc from Chile, despite what's written on the label. The problem is that many of Chile's Sauvignon vineyards have been found to contain a quite different variety called Sauvignonasse, which tastes similar when first made but which tires quickly, growing fruitless and flat in flavour. That said, a reputable winery should be providing hundred percent Sauvignon Blanc, and some Chilean examples are delicious, bone-dry and zippily fresh, with crisp gooseberry and lime and occasionally a slight savoury edge. The cool Casablanca Valley region makes some of the best wines. Go for Viña Casablanca, Mont Gras, Villard, and the good-value 35 South label.

**AUSTRALIA**  This is not a grape variety at which Australia excels. Winemakers there have tended to concentrate on Chardonnay and Semillon, leaving Sauvignon to their Kiwi neighbours. It is partly because many of Australia's top vineyard sites are simply too hot for Sauvignon, which needs a cooler touch if it is to remain racy and crisp. Still, the Australians are now looking to make more elegant wines alongside their traditional blockbusters, and so Sauvignon has become more popular among winemakers as they plant in cooler spots. The result is some impressive stuff, especially from Tasmania, Adelaide Hills and the Margaret River region south of Perth (where it is sometimes blended with Semillon). Try Lenswood, Katnook, Riddoch Sauvignons or Cullen's blend.

**USA**  The Californians have developed a unique type of Sauvignon and called it Fumé Blanc. This is oaked Sauvignon – so expect more richness, some creamy depths and sometimes a sweet note that will not be to everyone's taste. West Coast winemakers who first pushed this style had fine, oaked white Bordeaux in mind; unfortunately, too many Fumé Blancs lacked zippy acidity, dryness and the fruity stamp of Sauvignon. The style has been toned down of late – more of that bright, lively Sauvignon character is allowed to shine through, and there are certain Californian winemakers who don't use oak barrels at all for Sauvignon. But do tread carefully here until you establish that you like the Californian style! Washington State is the source of a few fruity, modern Sauvignons.

**REST OF EUROPE**  Bulgaria makes some reasonable Sauvignon Blanc, though overall quality is patchy. Hungary is a safer bet. This is a country which makes some super Sauvignon: dry, fresh, flavoursome and cheap, with tangy grapefruit and a often rather savoury, smoky note. Great for everyday quaffing. The south of France makes some Sauvignon in a richer, riper style than usual – the warm vineyards account for this.

## Storing and serving

The majority of the fruity, spicy whites need drinking up soon after purchase, as their wonderful aromas and vibrant flavours won't last more than a year. This applies especially to the more cheap and simple bottles like basic Irsai Oliver (see page 59). New Zealand Sauvignon is supposed to be consumed fairly young, but older bottles have proved delicious: full of tinned asparagus and baked greengage character. Cellar a top example, but drink up leaner, lesser wines within a year. Albariño and Pinot Blanc aren't great 'agers', either, so enjoy them while fairly young. But serious Alsace Gewürztraminer can be matured successfully for much longer – several years in bottle gives it a lovely mellow richness – although be warned that the blast of spice softens somewhat. This is one wine that can be enjoyed young or old, according to your taste.

# Gewürztraminer

It's hard to explain what the much-used term 'spicy white' means, but grab a glass of Gewürztraminer (or Gewürz, as this grape is often called) and the style immediately becomes clear. It's not hot, peppery chilli spice, of course, but an exotic, gingery appeal, with hints of rosewater, peach skin, dried apricots, sometimes a note of cardamon and often pink Turkish delight. Good Gewürz is headily perfumed, so the extraordinary, unique appeal of the wine assails you long before you get the liquid in your mouth. One sniff of a glass of Gewürz will tell you that here is something quite different. To be honest, it isn't for everyone, and even for its fans it probably isn't for quaffing every day – but Gewürz is fascinating stuff, and like all the spicy whites, it is a brilliant match for certain dishes; in this case I'd choose Thai spicy fish with loads of coriander and lemongrass, or even simple Chinese sweet-and-sour chicken.

**ALSACE AND THE REST OF EUROPE**  The most famous and best Gewurztraminers of all come from Alsace in eastern France – a region that has mastered premium, opulent but unoaked whites. These wines are full of fragrance and spice, richly golden-coloured and full in texture, often with a high thirteen percent alcohol, but they are not oaky, and a well-balanced example (as always with whites) should have crisp acidity to balance out that weight.

Wines from over fifty *grand cru* vineyard sites (named on the label) are supposed to be the best, but this isn't always the case and such wines can be an expensive disappointment. Avoiding sweetish wines (or indeed finding them, if you like a more honeyed style) can also prove tricky as there's little to help you on the label, but do note that the words *vendange tardive* or *sélection des grains nobles* do indicate sweet wine (see the section 'Sweet Wines' on pages 144–155). Poor Alsace Gewurz does exist, of course, often tasting 'flabby', lacking acidity and smelling like cheap perfume. To avoid this, pick a top producer like Hugel, Trimbach or Schlumberger or as an introduction, try a simpler but less expensive wine from a reliable cooperative winery like Turckheim or Ribeauvillé. Despite all these pitfalls – and the fact that Alsace Gewurz is often packaged in old-fashioned tall, green bottles with dense Gothic script on them – do give it a go as the wines can be quite brilliant, and among the most unusual and fascinating in the world.

In Germany, Gewürztraminer is considered much less important than Riesling. The wines are more simple, but prettily scented and often delicious. The best wines have a delightfully crisp finish; the worst taste a bit clumsy and unbalanced; German Gewürz never quite reaches the heights of Alsace Gewurz. Try a bottle from the Baden or Pfalz areas of the country. If you like Gewürz, trawl the shelves for bottles of the stuff from Eastern Europe (especially Hungary) and northern Italy, too – these can be a bargain and snappily fresh, although nothing touches Alsace.

**REST OF THE WORLD**  New Zealand is now producing some excellent Gewurztraminer, particularly from the cooler South Island vineyards of Marlborough. There's a delightful purity of fruit here – a clean citrus zest, tangerine note, perhaps with some lychee – and a dry, mineral quality to the best. Definitely worth a go if you see the Lawson's Dry Hills, Huia or Grove Mill labels. Australia produces very few Gewurzes of note as its vineyards are usually too hot for this variety, although the Piper's Brook winery in cool, breezy Tasmania makes a subtle, elegant wine. Chilean Gewürz, on the other hand, is successful, especially from the cool Casablanca Valley vineyards or the Bío-Bío region in the south. There aren't many around, but snap one up from Viña Casablanca, Undurraga or Cono Sur if you spot it. This wine doesn't crop up in California much, but a handful of decent wines come from Washington State.

## Matching fruity, spicy whites with food

The fruity, spicy whites described here are neither too overpowering on one hand, nor wimpy on the other, so they match a wide range of dishes, including simple chicken and fish. Pinot Blanc, for example, goes with lots of dishes, especially quiches, tarts and pizzas. The richer, fruity Sauvignons are great with asparagus, tomato and basil salad, and rich white fish and seafood dishes (fish in creamy sauce, fresh crab). Albariño is a wow with firm white fish, especially the hake often served in western Spain. Spicy whites are the ones to match with more exotic food – Gewürztraminer with mildly spicy, fragrant Thai dishes, or Chinese cuisine. Try a ultra-fruity Sauvignon or Gewürz with rich cheesy bakes or roast vegetables, as they both measure up well to hearty vegetarian fare.

# Other fruity, spicy whites

**Chenin Blanc** Drinkers of fruity, spicy whites usually like Chenin Blanc – when it's good, that is. This a difficult grape variety to fall in love with, partly because one of the two countries that makes a lot of it – South Africa – turns out so much commercial, off-dry wine from Chenin.

It's worth persevering with South African Chenin Blanc (somtimes known locally as Steen), though, as a superior bottle has a lovely juiciness to it, plenty of lime and guava flavours, nice rounded weight and a succulent finish. Better South African Chenins are moreish, crowd-pleasing wines, reasonably cheap and a great party white. Happily, the general standard is improving, and even supermarket own-labels are proving more reliable. The best producers are Mulderbosch (lightly oaked wine) and Nederburg, while KWV's Chenin is good value.

In France's Loire Valley, Chenin gets serious. This is where the amazingly long-lived Savennières is made entirely from Chenin; rapier-sharp with acidity when young, it achingly, slowly evolves into richer stuff with layers of ripe apple and cream over ten or twenty years in the cellar. Vouvray, too, can show Chenin Blanc at its best, with appley fruit again, and a hint of walnut oil (Vouvray can be dry, medium or sweet). Basic Loire whites made from this grape can be a real let-down, though. Humble Anjou Blanc is often over-sulphured and dilute in flavour, with a faint, wet-wool aroma, as if it's a jumper that has been left out in the rain. To be fair to this grape, it can produce impressive white wine when in the hands of a canny producer (Huët, Nicolas Joly) and it is a versatile beast, creating tasty sparkling and luscious sweet wines, so it gets a better press later on in this book.

**Pinot Blanc** It's hard to find anyone who actively dislikes Pinot Blanc. This grape produces wines which are easy-drinking, soft, fairly fruity in an appley sort of way, sometimes with a creamy quality and a note of almond oil or even peach kernel. It is really as a food wine that Pinot Blanc comes into its own, slipping down effortlessly with a wide range of savoury dishes. If you are dining in a crowd and you aren't sure which white wine to choose, plump for Pinot Blanc.

In Alsace, where arguably the best Pinot Blanc is made, the wine is served with onion tart, which makes a satisfying combination. There's something about the soft, almost earthy wine and highly flavoured vegetable dishes that works well. Josmeyer and Zind-Humbrecht make fine wines. Next best is to a try a lighter wine from Germany, where this variety is known as Weissburgunder.

**Albariño** Spain is much more famous for its fine red wines (from Rioja, and more recently Ribera and Navarra) than it is for whites, which at the cheaper end of the market can be decidedly plonk-like. But one serious white is made in the western extremes of the country. The Rías Baixas region of Galicia, on the Atlantic coast, is the source of a lovely dry white that oozes succulent, ripe orange and lime juice, has good rich weight, crisp acidity and no oak. Well chilled, it is a star match for white fish dishes. Exceptional labels include Lagar de Cervera and Pazo de Señoras. Expect quite high prices.

## Morio-Muskat and Irsai Oliver

These are the also-rans among spicy whites, after Gewürztraminer, that is. You won't get the depth of flavour or sheer excitement of an Alsace Gewürz here, but you should get something of that rosewater, lychee and ginger exoticism, and a crisp, fresh finish. Prices are low for both, so these grapes make an acceptable introduction to the spicy white style.

Morio-Muskat, which majors on the floral, scented character, is usually from Germany, while Irsai Oliver, which is usually snappy and dry with spicy peach flavour, hails from Slovenia or Hungary.

# shortcuts to success

## FIRST TASTE

• Sauvignon from the Loire Valley in France tastes much leaner than rich, ripe New Zealand Sauvignon, and South African styles sit somewhere in between, so make sure you know where your Sauvignon comes from. Don't expect them to taste the same just because they are made from the same grape variety Sauvignons vary a lot.

• Often called Fumé Blanc, oaked US Sauvignon has an almost sweet, vanilla note and will be richer and often less crisp. Fine, if you like that sort of thing, but be aware of it. White Bordeaux is sometimes oaky, too.

• Not everyone likes Gewürztraminer; people tend to either love or loathe the fruity, spicy whites. So it's a good idea to pick something else if you are trying to please a crowd.

• Do try these wines with food, and not just on their own, as these are the most consummately food-friendly of all the white wines.

## BUYER'S GUIDE

• You don't have to spend a fortune to get a decent fruity, spicy white. Trade up from the very cheapest and you'll hit a reasonably low price bracket where plenty of tangy, succulent flavour is delivered, particularly from the Sauvignon Blanc grape.

• It may cost a little more, but as long as you avoid the cult labels, New Zealand Sauvignon can be good value with loads of flavour, and is a reliable type of wine.

• Very cheap Gewurztraminer is worth avoiding – this is where the grape starts to smell and taste like floral air freshener! Hungary makes some bargain bottles of Gewurz; however, it's definitely worth splashing out on the best Gewurztraminer from Alsace once in a while.

• Chenin Blanc from South Africa is a safe bet for a party white – it is cheap, reliably tasty and fun, although pretty simple stuff. Poor examples from the Loire abound, but try a fine one from a top producer for a treat sometime, and discover Chenin at its best.

## MOVING ON

• If you love New Zealand Sauvignon, try other wines from different parts of this country. Most Sauvignon comes from Marlborough, so sample others from the Martinborough, Central Otago and Canterbury regions, too.

• Try blends of Sauvignon with Sémillon, as seen a great deal in the southwest of France. Most white Bordeaux is a blend of the two, and the pairing of these two grapes can be sensational.

• Like Gewurztraminer? Try other fruity, spicy whites – they are much more obscure but fascinating nonetheless. Irsai Oliver and Morio-Muskat should be on your shopping list.

• Rather than finding a wine to complement a dish, make some food especially to show off your fruity, spicy whites. These wines are fantastically good with Thai and Chinese dishes, so get your wok out and make a dish to match Gewurz.

# rich, oaky whites

Few people sit on the fence when it comes to drinking ripe, full-bodied white wines. Some love them, revelling in their powerful flavours and rich textures, while others find them too much and prefer their whites light and refreshing. Then there is the issue of oak-ageing. Some heavyweight white wines never see the inside of a barrel, but many others spend a long period maturing (and sometimes fermenting, too) in casks, and become even more strongly flavoured as a result of the toasted oaky character leaching into the wine. Opinion will always be divided on the heavily oaked white wines, but winemakers who are careful to balance the fruit, acid and oak elements so that nothing is overwhelming or out of kilter should always win plenty of fans.

Ten years ago, robust and hefty whites were all the rage. Wine-drinkers had grown tired of dilute, wimpy whites and the bright, fruit-driven styles arriving from warm vineyards in Australia and California were a welcome shock to the senses. Suddenly here were white wines bursting with generous, plump fruit and dripping with creamy oak. Then the inevitable backlash followed – we had had enough of these extroverts and longed for something more subtle. The good news is that nowadays there are rich whites with (generally speaking) better balance, more elegant flavours and crisper acidity to counteract those 'in-yer-face', bold fruit and oak flavours.

The key to enjoying our richest whites is to open them at a suitable moment. Blockbuster Chardonnays and Viogniers are not meant to be quaffed as crisp, light lunchtime aperitifs. But they do stand up to food well, and can make brilliant partners for luxury dishes such as smoked salmon pâté, succulent lobster, monkfish or even roast turkey and goose and all the trimmings. By contrast, a thin, weedy white would be totally overpowered by these dishes. So use your rich whites cleverly. Only roll out the big guns when the occasion is right. Hearty food, luxury feasts and cold weather all seem to make us want fleshier wines, much more so than with high summer, al fresco snacks. So if any white wines can be described as winter warmers, these are the ones!

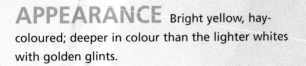

**APPEARANCE** Bright yellow, hay-coloured; deeper in colour than the lighter whites with golden glints.

**TEXTURE** Relatively rich and weighty, more viscous than the lighter whites, less so than the sweet whites.

# rich, oaky whites

AROMA Richly perfumed with hints of vanilla, cream, rich fruit (especially pineapples, peaches) perhaps buttered toast and hints of spicy wood from fermenting and/or ageing in oak barrels. Some (e.g. Viognier) have a heavy floral, honeysuckle-and-lilies perfume.

FLAVOUR Full and fruity, fairly viscous and weighty in texture for a dry white. Fruit flavours include ripe oranges, peaches, apricots, pineapples, mangos. Buttery, creamy undertones, occasionally a distinct nuttiness. Lightly oaked wines have subtle roundness and layer of vanilla; heavily oaked ones carry more toasty, sawdusty character. Some older wines take on a honeyed, bees-wax note while remaining dry. Lingering, full after-taste.

# Chardonnay

For many people, rich, ripe and powerful white wine means only one thing: the Chardonnay grape. Take top-quality Chardonnay grapes and ferment them in new-oak barrels, leaving the wine to age there awhile, and the result can be a supremely sophisticated and complex wine, for many the most exciting white wine in the world. And it packs a flavoursome punch. Chardonnay occasionally produces light, bland wine but not often – that's one reason why winemakers across the globe like growing it. That, and the fact that they can mould it anyway they like, as Chardonnay is easy to work with (it grows well and likes oak-ageing, for example). With plenty of ripe citrus and tropical fruit, tempting notes of toasted hazelnuts, peach kernels, buttered brioche and cream, top examples are some of the most satisfying and wonderful whites ever made.

**FRANCE** To taste the very best, splash out on a fine example from the Burgundy region of France. White burgundy is almost always made from Chardonnay, although it won't say so on the label – as in many French classic wine regions, the Burgundians don't advertise their grape varieties, instead they focus on the village or individual vineyard where the wine was made. Other white grapes like Aligoté, Pinot Blanc and Pinot Gris are also grown in Burgundy, but these are relative rarities and you can be certain that if you buy mainstream white burgundy you are getting a bottle of Chardonnay.

Indeed, if you splash out on some of the premium wines that come from Burgundy's prize locations along the Côte d'Or – most come from the the southern Côte de Beaune area between Aloxe-Corton and Santenay – you should see what first-rate Chardonnay can achieve: opulent, remarkably concentrated, yet beautifully fresh and well-balanced wine, the oaky hints enhancing, not overpowering, that gorgeous, mouth-filling, honeyed-yet-dry fruit. Wines to try – and don't forget these names refer to the location not the producer or grape variety – include those hailing from the villages of Meursault, Puligny-Montrachet, Chassagne-Montrachet, Aloxe-Corton, with the first-rate vineyard areas including Le Montrachet, Bâtard-Montrachet and Corton-Charlemagne. The best bottles age well, too, losing any hard edges and mellowing out to become wonderfully well-knit,

the softer acidity and fruit binding seamlessly with the nutty, creamy oak.

Or that's the idea, anyway. Burgundy is a frustratingly difficult and patchy wine region, with big differences between fine and poor vintages, and plenty of inferior wine as well as those true stars. Even burgundy connoisseurs acknowledge that quality can be uneven, for whites as well as reds. Since the best wines are so expensive, it's important to pick a top producer and mug up on the good years. For the record, 1996, 1997 and 2000 were all good. Try to spend a bit extra now and again and sample fairly pricey white burgundy, as it only gets great once it gets expensive. This is partly because all the top vineyards (classified as *grands crus*, the great growths – the top spots – followed by the *premiers crus* areas) can only produce a small amount of wine, and international demand is, of course, high. But these are wines well worth saving up for. Top producers of fine burgundy include Coche-Dury, Joseph Drouhin, Louis Jadot, Jobard, Domaine Leflaive and Verget.

Trawl around the cheaper white burgundies and, sadly, you will be in for a few disappointments, especially if you have sampled the great and glorious of the region. Those from the Côte Chalonnais, such as Montagny, Rully and Mercurey, can be reasonably good value, offering fresh, quality white at a less-scary price than the Côte d'Or. But the Chardonnays from the vast vineyards of the Mâcon area are unreliable; basic Mâcon Blanc in particular is a dodgy way to part with your money and can taste thin and raw. Do try burgundies labelled Pouilly-Fuissé, though, from a superior part of the Mâcon – they are often satisfyingly creamy and rich, and St-Véran provides some decent, good-value stuff in the mid-price bracket. And basic, generic Bourgogne Blanc from a top winemaker can be surprisingly good: fresh, fruity, juicy and ripe.

Chablis, a famous white-wine area in the north of the Burgundy region, traditionally makes wine that is a little lighter in style, partly because it has slightly cooler vineyards. In some parts of Chablis, the soil is rich in chalk and clay, and traditionalists believe the best wines are made from Chardonnay grown on these sites (the soil is known as Kimmeridgian). Chablis is often described as having a steely quality – it certainly tastes a little leaner, more crisp, even with a more mineral edge, than other white burgundies. It is also more lightly oaked, even sometimes unoaked. As such, it perhaps belongs in our fruity whites section – except that in recent times more rich and rounded, ultra-fruity Chablis has been appearing. Expect warm, tangy hints of apple, orange and even rhubarb. This wine is not a true heavyweight, then, but rather represents the lighter face of Chardonnay, albeit with that characteristically generous fruit. Pick a Chablis from one of the *grands crus* (great growths, see above) of the region – there are seven: Blanchots, Bougros, Les Clos, Grenouilles, Preuses, Valmur, Vaudésir – or from one of the more numerous *premiers crus*, the next step down. Quality in Chablis, by the way, is thankfully more reliable than in other parts of Burgundy.

For simpler joys, with less chance of a severe disappointment but admittedly fewer high points, try Chardonnays from other parts of France. In particular, fans of rich, oaky white wine won't want to miss the buttery, generous Chardonnays of the deep south of

## Making the difference

Some oaky white wines are fermented in small barrels (called *barriques* in France), and left to age there. Others are simply aged in the barrels after fermentation in tanks. French and American oak are the most commonly used for reds and whites – American oak gives a more overt vanilla flavour than French. A cheaper method of getting some oak flavour into wine is to soak oak chips in a vat of wine. This is perfectly legal (although it gives a cruder flavour than barrels), but the use of laboratory-concocted oak essence is generally not allowed.

France. These wines (often labelled Vins de Pays d'Oc, or country wines of the Languedoc), really do seem to taste sunny, exuding the warmth of the Southern vineyards, which creates super-ripe Chardonnay grapes. But they are 'identikit' wines, tasting mainly very similar to one another and hardly reflecting *terroir* (the character of an individual site) in the same way decent burgundy does.

Most of these southern belles are aged in oak barrels or by using oak chips (see page 67). A few are blends, but mostly they are one hundred percent Chardonnay. You know what you are getting here; not only is it much more likely to say Chardonnay on the label, but you can pretty much guarantee succulent pineapple and peachiness, buttery-toasty hints, and a rich, satisfyingly full finish. They are much more reliable than basic white burgundy, but don't expect great complexity or excitement. They taste a lot like Chardonnay from newer wine-making countries – one reason why the south of France has been dubbed the 'New, New World'.

**AUSTRALIA** Which brings us to the second most famous Chardonnay-producing country in the world. Down Under, in Australia's warm vineyards, an ultra-rich, wonderfully concentrated, luxuriously ripe form of Chardonnay has proved extremely popular around the world. It used to be almost too much, leaving you with a mouthful of sawdust and vanilla. 'Blockbuster' was the word used to describe the heftiest, chunkiest Australian Chardonnays from hot areas like Hunter Valley in New South Wales, and the Barossa Valley near Adelaide.

These wines certainly wowed us on first taste (they first arrived in significant numbers in the 1980s). If you had only ever sipped bland, weak, light white wines such as Muscadet and Liebfraumilch, Australian Chardonnay was a shock to the senses. What a blast of ripe, tropical fruit! What a rich perfume! What a dollop of vanilla and spice from all that fresh, resinous new oak! The problem is that, like most extroverts, the loudest wines get a bit tiresome after a while. They are so heavy and gloopy, it's as though you should scoop them up with a spoon, not knock them back at a party. They don't seem subtle and refreshing enough. So, recently the Aussies have started making slightly more elegant wines. They age them in oak for less time, or they use older, less resinous oak, or they don't use wood at all, making their wines entirely in stainless-steel containers. And they sometimes source their grapes from cooler sites where the flavours don't get so overblown and where the acidity has more bite.

Among the cool-climate areas to look out for (helpfully, the Australians spell these out on a label) are the island of Tasmania, off the south coast of the mainland, the Adelaide Hills and Clare Valley regions in South Australia, and Mornington Peninsula and Yarra Valley in Victoria. Expect wines from these areas to taste more crisp and elegant than wines from warmer spots, although, with the exception of the ultra-fresh Tassie wines, they still retain plenty of broad, ripe Aussie fruit. Top producers include Piper's Brook, Petaluma, Lenswood, Tarrawarra and Grosset. But despite the rise of such relatively cool-climate wines, baking regions such as the Barossa Valley and Hunter Valley are still putting out heftier, chunkier styles, and the Margaret River in Western Australia is coming up with a refined Chardonnay style that lies somewhere in between. Try the Cullen, Leeuwin Estate or Cape Mentelle labels from the latter.

The fact is, today some very rich Australian Chardonnays are still around, and they are great with food such as the creamiest fish sauces, the most luxurious lobster, smoked salmon or roast turkey. But they're too much on their own as aperitifs. The new lighter styles (still big, but not *so* big) are more balanced, fresher, more thirst-quenching, more restrained. The latest trend is towards regional characteristics, Burgundy-style, so watch out for some marked differences in wines from the far-flung Aussie wines regions. Try a few to see which suits you best.

Blends of Chardonnay with the Semillon grape are common in Australia. These are no great shakes, almost seeming like a watered-down version of the straight Chardonnays. But they are generally clean, bright and have enough sunny fruit. Their prices are low too. They make appealing crowd-pleasers, and usually go down well at a party.

REST OF THE WORLD  In California, it has been a similar story with Chardonnay. The West Coast winemakers used to make hugely successful, monster Chardonnay that you could almost cut with a knife, but they are now turning to a more subtle style and growing grapes in cooler vineyard areas for their more restrained flavours and fresher streaks of acidity. The best examples now rival anything made in France and Australia, although they are mightily expensive.

At the cheaper end, California Chardonnay can taste a bit over-oaky, sweet and bland. Not really to everyone's taste, especially if you are used to drinking more sophisticated fare! In between lie some impressive Chardonnays, fairly full-on in character and also heavily oaked, but better balanced by riper concentrated pineapple and peach flavours, and a crisp finish. And do splash out on those premium West Coast wines once in a while – they are sublime, they age well for years, and are a must for all those who love big whites. Try examples from the Carneros region, Russian River or the Sonoma Coast for poised, nicely balanced bottles. Top names include Beringer, Hess, Kistler, Saintsbury and Au Bon Climat. Avoid the very big, inexpensive brands.

South Africa is rapidly catching up, making newly impressive Chardonnays. The Western Cape's wineries, which fell behind the times during apartheid and an estranged overseas market, have been a long time catching up, but today anyone who is a fan of the upfront and oaky style of white wine should give Cape Chardonnay a go – look for ones from the Robertson, Stellenbosch and Paarl regions for a taste

of the best from names such as Vergelegen, Rustenberg or Danie de Wet. These wines are typically rich and no-nonsense examples, but with well-controlled rounded oak structure.

New Zealand is another source of fine Chardonnay. Its warmer areas (Gisborne and Hawke's Bay on the North Island) produce richer wines with a tropical-fruit edge; the cooler spots like Marlborough on the South Island, make a crisper, more citric version, but they are all typically packed with a juicy, pure flavour. Perhaps because of the fame of New Zealand's Sauvignon Blanc, its Chardonnay has often been forgotten in the rush, so don't miss out. Some of the most important wineries (Villa Maria, Te Mata, Sileni, Palliser, Hunter's, Cloudy Bay) make excellent Chardonnays. Try to sample wines from different regions, including Martinborough on the North Island and Central Otago on the South, if you can.

Then there's South America, and Chile, origin of such good-value Chardonnay. If you want lots of fruit for your money, and a reliable source of fresh, clean white with a nicely judged edge of oak, give Chilean Chardonnay a whirl. There are a few super-premium, more pricey Chilean wines around, too, which prove that the country can make top stuff too. And go for the new kid on the Chardonnay block: Argentina, now impressing us with its new, highly modern, bright and big Chardonnays at heart-warmingly low prices.

REST OF WORLD  Don't be fooled into thinking that Europe's only Chardonnay stronghold is France – even though the shop shelves are usually groaning with French examples. In fact, if you like plump, rich Chardonnay, you should look into the bastion of good-value bottles that is Eastern Europe. Bulgaria and Hungary both turn out reasonably good, clean and tasty versions; nothing very special, but since they are cheap, they're fine for everyday quaffing. Don't expect anything fantastically rich and powerful, however. Soft, fruity and simple is the name of the game here.

In Italy, however, things get more serious with the richly oaked premium wines made in Tuscany, and the highly modern, Aussie taste-alikes from the hot vineyards of Sicily. Spain and Portugal major in other styles of wine, but there are still a few well-made, almost-serious, oaked Chardonnays about. One surprising source of high-class, judiciously oaked Chardonnay is Austria. The Austrians sometimes call this grape Morillon, and best examples come from the Wachau and Styria regions. These little-known gems are a rarity on the export market – if you see one, snap it up! Even rarer outside its country of origin is Canadian Chardonnay but that, too, can be serious stuff with incisive acidity to balance the richness. And if you see one of China's big, oaked Chardonnays, give it a whirl; a small handful are now being exported, appearing mainly in Chinese restaurants worldwide.

# Sémillon

Sometimes blended with Chardonnay to create limey, buttery, rounded white wines, Sémillon deserves a listing on its own for the weighty, toasty, almost smoky wines made from it in newer wine-making countries. Sémillon is interesting – it's a chameleon-like grape. Sometimes it makes lean, grassy whites that would be out of place in this style section, but when it's ripe, mature and sometimes oak-aged, it certainly falls into the 'rich whites' category. Then it makes just about the best dessert wines in the world as well (see the section 'Sweet Wines' on pages 144–155). A versatile beast, then.

**AUSTRALIA AND REST OF THE WORLD** If it's big and loud, 'in-yer-face' Semillon you're after, head to Australia and in particular the Hunter Valley (NSW) and the Clare and Barossa Valleys (South Australia) for sun-baked, so-ripe-they're-almost-sweet wines which are packed with sumptuous flavours of preserved lemons, honey, angelica and lime. Especially lime.

Admittedly, the wines don't often taste like that at the very beginnning. They have a more grassy, lean character, although that lime juice usually makes them succulent and characterful. But after a few years in bottle, Semillon comes over all toasty and rich, as if spread with lime marmalade and honeycomb, yet strangely still dry.

It's seriously attractive wine, Semillon, and if you're bored with oaky Chardonnay but still hanker after a full-on flavour, make it your next stop. Despite its appeal, this is an underrated style of wine, set to become more popular as the craze for Chardonnay wears off. Not all great Semillons are made in Australia, by the way – a few worthwhile ones are now being made in South Africa and Argentina, too.

**BORDEAUX** Sémillon from Bordeaux can be extraordinarily good: rounded and weighty, with lemony freshness, and again, that honeyed, almost smokey/nutty appeal once aged. It's often blended with the zestier Sauvignon Blanc and aged in oak barrels to add extra depth and flavour. The top white Bordeaux in this style can be a knock-out, but be prepared to shell out for it. Oh, and you'll need a good cellar as they take a long time in bottle to mellow out and reach their best.

As with Chardonnay in Burgundy, they don't put 'Sémillon' on the label in Bordeaux, but many whites from the area contain this grape. Not all, however, will be rich and flavoursome. In fact, a lot of cheap white Bordeaux is dilute and tart. Go for the glorious châteaux of Graves and Pessac-Léognan if you want to taste the most serious and exciting.

## Matching rich, oaky whites with food

Rich, dry whites demand food. They are not the best wines to choose as aperitifs because they are too powerful. Instead, pair them with roast poultry, chicken in creamy sauces, and full-flavoured fish and seafood such as salmon, crab and lobster. Oaky Chardonnays are great with smoked salmon as the wood flavours chime in with the smokiness. Peachy Viognier is an impressive partner for creamy, mild curries. If you want to pair white wine with meat (pork, beef in creamy sauces), go for the powerful wine described in this section, not light, dry whites.

### Blends

Not all rich, oaky whites are made from one hundred percent
of one grape. Others are a blend of grapes, such as Semillon-
Chardonnay blends from Australia. These popular wines are
reliable, clean, soft and fruity – a little one-dimensional
perhaps, but great value at parties when everyone should
enjoy their fruity appeal. Then there's the blend of Roussanne
and Marsanne in the Rhône Valley, and the winning
combination of Sémillon and leaner, grassier Sauvignon Blanc
in Bordeaux. Wine-lovers seem particularly keen on single
varieties at the moment, but do try blends as well. They are
not necessarily any better, but neither are they any worse.

# Viognier

For every fan of perfumed, heady, full-bodied white, wines made from the Viognier grape are a must. And for every fashion-conscious wine-lover, Viognier is currently top of the list.

**FRANCE** All grapes from France's Rhône Valley seem to be enjoying a vogue, and that's where this exotic white vine comes from. Viognier (it's pronounced Vee-on-yeh) is seriously cool in wine-drinking circles right now. Which is a good thing when you get your hands on an impressive bottle of the stuff, and a big disappointment when you come across a dud.

The problem with Viognier, you see, is that if it's made properly, with low-yielding vines, and thus concentrated grapes, and careful work in the winery, it is sublime: a lingering mouthful of squashy ripe peaches, dried apricots, with a gorgeous fragrance of honeysuckle and white blossom. Nothing else quite conjures up heady late summer so well.

But, sadly, there are lots of dilute versions around which don't have much perfume, and which are insipid or taste of artificial pear-drops. These have simply been made from vines with high yields of grapes, which may be fine for the grower who wants to sell a lot of fruit, but means that the resulting wine lacks that all-important perfumed peachiness. Sometimes a flabby and disappointing Viognier means it has become too ripe, losing its crispness and concentration. You get the picture – Viognier needs attention in the vineyard and it is not always great, although when you catch the scent of a good one, you'll see what all the fuss is about.

To make sure you get all that natural peachy fruit and lovely aroma, pick one from the Condrieu area of the Rhône. These wines are opulent, intense and heady… and extremely expensive. The south of France, especially the Languedoc, makes cheaper, less concentrated versions. These offer a reasonable introduction to Viognier, but do avoid the bargain-basement ones which can be flabby (lacking acidity) and disappointingly dull.

**REST OF THE WORLD** Since Viognier became so sought-after, it hasn't been a surprise to see the newer wine-producing countries start to have a go at it. Most successful is the US, where decent rich wines with firm, crisp acidity are being produced in California. You might come across one or two fairly well-made Viogniers from Argentina, Australia and South Africa, too. Seek them out. They will be fruit-driven, packed with peaches and held together with a creamy seam of oak. Expect more Viogniers to appear on the scene since this grape is so much in vogue. And of course, because winemakers love a challenge!

# Other rich, oaky whites

**Roussanne and Marsanne** The unusual flavours of these wines are increasingly appreciated. They will appeal to anyone who likes their wines forward and full, but is tired of those modern, bright, 'fruit-salad' styles of white.

They may not be famous (yet), but this duo of grapes is responsible for the much-loved white wines of the Rhône, like St-Péray, Crozes-Hermitage and St-Joseph. These wines are not fresh and fruity in the way that Viognier is; they are full-bodied and waxy, weighty, with a deep colour and flavours of nut oil, peach kernel, spice and sometimes aniseed. With age they grow honeyed. Intrigued? Then try these white Rhônes. They go particularly well with savoury food. These are not wines to enjoy on their own as they taste too heavy and lacking in crisp fruit, but match them with fish or chicken in creamy or cheesy sauces and they come into their own.

Not much is made from these grapes around the world, but watch this space. Winemakers in Australia and California in particular are intrigued by the unusual flavours of Rhône whites, and are trying to make their own versions. A few (very oaky) Marsannes are already making an appearance and it's only a matter of time before more hit the shelves. You might come across a big, aromatic Marsanne from the south of France in the meantime.

**Pinot Gris** This grape is very rarely oaked, but choose the right label and you can have another full-on, rich white wine.

Okay, so Pinot Grigio, as the Italians call it, is anything but rich, and this grape is very rarely oaked. But try the version of Pinot Gris made in Alsace, in eastern France, and bingo! You've got another full-on white wine. The grape is often called Tokay-Pinot Gris here, although it has nothing to do with the sweet wine called Tokay made in Hungary. Here we're talking about a rounded, almost fat white wine, that looks thickly textured in the glass, and is mouth-filling and weighty on the palate. It smells and tastes smoky, spicy, orangey, dry yet ripe, and it is great with rich food such as smooth pâté, confit de canard, roast goose. Not a wishy-washy wine at all, and a million miles away in style from other crisp, light Pinot Gris made around the world (for more on these see the section 'Light, Dry Whites' on pages 36–49).

**Viura/Malvasia** No chapter on rich whites would be complete without mention of one of the most rich, sultry and heavily oaked dry wines of all time: classic white Rioja.

Made in the north of Spain mainly from the local Viura grape, with the help of Malvasia and Garnacho Blanco grapes in the blend, this is a wine that won't please everyone. Deep yellow, waxily thick, reeking of wood and sawdust, and tasting of vanilla and cream, traditional white Rioja rests in barrel for years to take on such a big oak influence. It's a classic, old-fashioned style of wine, nowadays winning fewer fans as people expect brighter, younger, fresh fruit flavours. Do give it a try, though – not on its own, as it seems heavy and lumbering like that, but matched with creamy, savoury dishes or smoked fish, which will stand up to the oaky wine nicely and complement it.

Sadly, this style of Rioja is being replaced to an extent by a younger, leaner, crisper style in the modern era. Shame – we need all the different styles of wine the world can give us if we are not to sink into uniformity.

## Serving and storing

Serve all dry whites, including these blockbusters, well-chilled, straight from the fridge, and keep them cold with an ice bucket. Splash them into large-bowled glasses – perhaps red wine glasses– filling them only halfway up so you can swirl the liquid easily and savour its heady aroma. All powerful whites should be pleasant to drink on release, and don't necessarily need cellaring. Simple wines like basic Chardonnays, cheap Viogniers and blends of Sémillon/ Chardonnay need opening quickly after purchase. But top Chardonnays will mellow out and grow more attractive, soft and integrated with a couple of years' age, and top burgundies grow wonderfully rounded, inviting and nutty with maturity. Don't miss older Australian Semillon, too – it's quite different from the younger stuff: honeyed, toasty and rich. Store all wines in a cool, dark place on their sides.

# shortcuts to success

## FIRST TASTE

- Don't expect simple refreshment here. The rich, oaky whites should be packed with flavour, probably laced with toasty oak, and with a lingering finish. Not for the faint-hearted!

- Don't slp a heavily oaked, powerful white wine on a hot summer's day in the garden; it isn't a mere thirst-quencher and will taste too heavy. Save rich, oaky whites for matching with rich, savoury food dishes.

- The best powerful whites are those with fine balance. They have a fresh, crisp acidity running through them, which lifts all that ripeness and rich oak. Look out for these sorts of wines as you will enjoy them better if you're drinking more than one glassfull.

- You don't have to tolerate oakiness to get a rich white as plenty of these wines are made without oak-ageing. Try a Viognier or a mature Sémillon that has not been oaked, or an unoaked Aussie Chardonnay.

- But fans of the ultra-oaky styles should try traditional white Rioja – it's as vanilla-packed as wine gets…

- If you prefer something crisper overall but enjoy the rich fruitiness of grapes like Chardonnay, pick a Chardonnay from a cooler climate, like Tasmania or Adelaide Hills in Australia, or Chablis from Burgundy in France, where the acidity levels in the grapes are somewhat higher.

## BUYER'S GUIDE

• The best-value rich whites are southern French Chardonnays and those from Chile. Hungarian ones can be a bargain, and South Africa offers more serious stuff at a decent price. Don't buy the very cheapest white burgundy as it is patchy in quality, and tread carefully among the lower-priced Californians.

• At the higher end of the price scale, top burgundies, Viogniers from the Rhône, and the best labels from Australia and California are as good as it gets in this style category. Do try to splash out on them now and again to see what the very best of this style can be like.

• Don't give in to fashion. If you love the older styles of very oaky Aussie Chardonnay, then fine. Or if you dislike ultra-trendy Viognier, then don't drink it! It's your choice, and the rich, oaky whites have always swung in and out of fashion more than other types of wine as they are extrovert styles and some people get tired of them. Stick to what you like – regardless of trends!

• Know your oak, whether it's to avoid it or to search out oaky whites. Look for words such as barrel-fermented or *barrique/chêne* (France) or *crianza* (Spain) on a label to indicate ageing in oak casks. Some lighter Chardonnays might state that they are unoaked or lightly oaked, which all helps you to choose a style you like.

## MOVING ON

• Don't just stick to Chardonnay. Not all the best rich whites are made from this one famous grape variety. Try some of the other grapes recommended in this section; that way you won't get bored with just one set of flavours. What about Sémillon, Viognier or Marsanne?

• And if you do buy a lot of Chardonnay, be sure to try lots of different bottles. Not all Chardonnay tastes the same, by any means. Go for a new region, a new producer, an older wine or one with a less oaky character. Don't get stuck in a rut! Some other Chardonnay styles are discussed in the section on 'Sparkling Wines' (see pages 130–143).

• Try blends of grapes, too – Chardonnay with Sémillon, or Roussanne with Marsanne. Don't stick to single-varietal wines alone.

• The rich, oaky whites can get tiresome – too loud and overpowering – if you don't make sure to buy relatively fresh and well-balanced wines, match them with the correct food, and ring the changes with other types of wine regularly. Investigate them thoroughly, and if you are getting bored, that's the time to treat yourself to a top burgundy or southern-hemisphere Chardonnay, or a Condrieu, to remind yourself just how fabulous rich, oaky whites can sometimes be!

# light and smooth reds

The most famous light red of all is Beaujolais, a wine which at best is joyfully summery, scented and fruity, packed with soft, tangy strawberries, but which all too often tastes tart and characterless. Yes, bad Beaujolais is a serious turn-off, especially in these days of reliable, juicy, warm-climate wines. Recently it seems heavyweight wines have swept us off our feet – think Châteauneuf-du-Pape or California Cabernet – with the unfortunate result that some delightfully seductive and subtle reds described on the next few pages have become overlooked. Don't make this mistake. There are certain key wine-drinking moments when a light and/or smooth red is the better choice by far, just as long as you select wisely.

For example, do you really want a big, blockbuster Aussie Shiraz or spicy, full-on Rhône red when you're sitting outside in hot weather, eating delicate summer dishes? I didn't think so. This is decidedly the occasion for a more restrained smoothie like Pinot Noir or a cool-climate Cabernet Franc. If your palate is fatigued from ultra-ripe fruit and heavy tannins, they are exactly what you should turn to. Don't be afraid to chill these wines a little, either; a touch of cold emphasises their refreshing, cherry-berry succulence.

Strictly speaking, not all the wines discussed here are 'light'. Pinot Noir gives a certain impression of being light, as it is soft and gentle as a baby's skin. But it can also be concentrated in its fruitiness, and have beguiling, intense layers of chocolate, nuts and even cream. So 'smooth' is the adjective that applies here, rather than light. Gamay, the Beaujolais grape, often produces trite, weakling wines, like Beaujolais Nouveau, but the finest Beaujolais crus ('growths') from the best sites have an admirable depth of flavour, plushy and lingering, rather than tough and tannic. So think refreshing and mellow in the case of the most tempting wines that follow. Not necessary featherweight, but with a certain lightness of touch.

**APPEARANCE** Less concentrated and densely coloured than the rich, tannic reds. Expect a bright red-garnet colour, not the black-purple intensity of heftier wines. Very young bottles sometimes have a bluish tinge; older ones are more brick-coloured.

**TEXTURE** Think soft and juicy, silky and mellow, without the heavy tannins of richer reds. The lightest, leanest wines taste insubstantial, jammy, even thin, while a fine burgundy should be velvet-smooth, ripe and rounded.

# light and smooth reds

AROMA  A high-summer perfume of fresh red berries is often found, especially strawberries, although sniff for raspberries, red cherries, cranberries and plums, too. Loire reds have a leafy character and perhaps a hint of green capsicum. Beaujolais can have an estery aroma of pear-drops or banana chews; underripe wines sometimes smell of green beans and mown grass.

FLAVOUR  Those red-berry fruits again, fresh and squishily ripe. There are sometimes hints of earth, game and spice in older burgundies, some say even stables and horse manure! Look out for layers of chocolate, coffee and toasted nuts, too.

# Pinot Noir

It's not always light by any means, but Pinot Noir is (or should be) wonderfully smooth, silky and soft as crushed velvet. This is one of the greatest red grapes in the world, producing wines with a lovely, lush strawberry perfume and flavour when young, which gradually mature into more farmyardy, gamey depths. It is also one of the most difficult vines of all, requiring much tender, loving care and sensitivity in the vineyard and winery unless it is to go horribly wrong and produce an insipid, jammy stew. So for many ambitious winemakers, Pinot Noir is the holy grail– they are determined to master such a pernickety variety and make a show-stopping red from it.

So how do they make great Pinot Noir? This is a thin-skinned grape which succumbs easily to rot and disease, so the right conditions are crucial. It needs the correct soils (limestone is a plus), reasonably dry conditions (dampness is a minus) and the grape-growers must watch their yields very carefully, keeping them low if they want to avoid producing a wine that is too dilute. Although winemakers across the globe strive hard to get it right, the best wines arguably still come from Burgundy, in France, where winemakers have had centuries of experience with this temperamental vine. Plenty of basic (and not so basic) burgundy is poor, but the top wines are sublime, as we shall see below. Other countries that are getting the better of this grape are the United States, Chile and New Zealand. If you've had a bad experience with Pinot Noir, don't give up on it, as when this grape is good, it is very good indeed, with a complexity, concentration and soft, sexy gorgeousness unrivalled by any of the other smooth, light reds. Just tread very carefully!

**FRANCE**  Pinot Noir isn't found in vast numbers across the French winemaking regions; instead it is concentrated in two or three. The most important, of course, is Burgundy. Put simply, white burgundy is all about Chardonnay, and red burgundy is all about Pinot Noir. Sure, a little wine is made from other red grapes in Burgundy, but Pinot Noir is what wine-lovers really want from this region: Pinot Noir that is sensual, perfumed and luscious, almost sweet with ripe fruitiness.

Sounds great, doesn't it? But here's a warning: to bag a truly super bottle and avoid the cheap, tart stuff, you need to know a bit about burgundy and it is *not* an easy subject to get to grips with. Some burgundy buffs devote their whole lives to unravelling the wines of this complex corner of France. This is partly because the area is split up into a patchwork of different small vineyards. Conscientious winemakers sweat to extract the individual character of each plot of land, imparting a sense of it in the finished wine. The French refer to this as *terroir* – the site, soil, sun, rainfall, slope – defining the quality and nature of the finished wine (see also page 17). It's the opposite of the large-scale southern-hemisphere, vine-growing region where an ocean of identical liquid flows from the same enormous tract of land. In Burgundy, Pinot Noir is crafted from minute nooks and crannies, and to understand it properly, you need to get to know the area, its villages, its most important vineyards, and the characteristics of the individual wines made in them. In fact, to become a real burgundy aficionado, you should visit the region and drive around, getting a feel of the land.

For those who want to appreciate red burgundy from their armchair, do be aware that the name of the place within the region, and even the specific vineyard site, is considered extremely important here. There are over one hundred appellations, ranging from generics like Bourgogne Rouge to the acclaimed *grands crus* that can be less than one hectare in size. Let's break them down into digestible nuggets of information:

there are twenty-four sites designated *grands crus*, or best 'growths', for red wine, all in the Côte de Nuits except one: Corton. Then there are dozens of *premiers crus*, the next step down the ladder for top vineyard sites. All the *grand cru* and *premier cru* vineyards are named on the label. Blends of wines from *premier cru* sites are labelled '*premier cru*' rather than with the name of an individual site, and then there are wines from specific villages such as Givry or Chambolle-Musigny. At the bottom of the ladder are the simple Bourgogne Rouge and the even more basic Bourgogne Grand Ordinaire.

Of course, the producers are important, although you would be forgiven for thinking that Burgundy was entirely about parcels of land, not winemakers. Some of the best Burgundian names to sample are Joseph Drouhin, Domaine Leroy, Louis Jadot and Domaine de la Romanée-Conti. Prices are certainly on the high side. It should be said that red burgundy only becomes reliable once you ignore the bargain basement. In fact, it only becomes interesting and worthwhile once prices are steep. If all the above were not enough to put off the everyday tippler, this is a region of highly

variable vintages, so only pick wines from a fine year – 1999, 1996, 1995, 1993 or 1990 – rather than a rotten one.

Some Pinot Noir is also grown in the Loire Valley where it is notable for red Sancerre. There is another source of Pinot in France, and that's Alsace, in the eastern extremes of the country. This is a region renowned for white wines, with Pinot Noir its solitary red of any significance. The wines tend to be straightforward, fruity and light, with a wild strawberry perfume and flavour but little complexity. They are at their best served lightly chilled in the summer with fresh salmon: a rare, tasty partnership of red wine and fish.

**REST OF THE WORLD** Non-European winemakers struggle gamefully with Pinot Noir, usually looking to the magnificent wines of Burgundy as benchmarks and hoping to emulate them, or make a different but equally great version of their own. They don't always get it right by any means; a sweetish, red-berryish, lightish red of no distinction is more often the result, and frankly, that's a disappointment from such a potentially fascinating grape. Still, warmer-climate

## Making the difference
Carbonic maceration is the technical term for the traditional method of making Beaujolais (see page 84). Instead of crushing the grapes, winemakers leave the bunches of grapes to ferment whole in vats, until they collapse and give up their juice. This gives a soft, juicy style of wine, as the tannins that are released from crushed skins, stalks and pips do not appear to such a great degree as in other red wines.

Pinot is gradually becoming better as grape-growers and winemakers are getting to grips with this quixotic vine. Sometimes the wines from Oregon impress. The state was heralded as Pinot's 'second home' for a long time in the 1980s, then inconsistent quality and some poor vintages made critics think twice, but Oregon can still come up with the goods (try Domaine Drouhin, Erath Vineyards and Firesteed). Shame the wines are not cheaper, or more widely available. California has some success with the grape if it is planted in areas like Carneros, Russian River and Santa Barbara, where the hot sun is cooled by ocean breezes. Saintsbury, Au Bon Climat and Calera are producers to watch.

New Zealand has recently made a big splash with its Pinot, and certainly some fine examples have come out of Marlborough, Central Otago and Martinborough, but while Kiwi Pinot is fairly reliable, it is also a little simple and one-dimensional. Martinborough Vineyards, Isabel Estate, Rippon and Mount Difficulty are among the best names. South Africa has one or two elegant wines (look out for the Walker Bay/Hermanus area for these), and Chile can provide good-value Pinot, bursting with cherry-berry fruit and perhaps a little smooth chocolate. Back in Europe, Romania is the underdog that triumphs, now and again, with cheap but decidedly cheerful Pinot, particularly from the Dealul Mare region. And Germany is another surprising source of palatable Pinot, more successful in the Pfalz and Baden regions than anywhere else. Here this grape is known as Spätburgunder.

# Gamay (Beaujolais)

It makes sense to deal with the Gamay grape next, because it is the grape responsible for Beaujolais, and Beaujolais is made just south of Burgundy. For true wine buffs, Beaujolais will never rival burgundy, but it remains a much-loved red, and can be wonderfully fruity, super-smooth and juicy, with the unmistakeable flavour of fresh red berries – summer pudding in a glass. Gamay has been aptly described as the jester to king Pinot Noir: more light-hearted, easygoing, frivolous. Don't take Beaujolais too seriously, is the message, but don't dismiss it, either. It's one of the best reds to drink without food, as its moreish, succulent character means it slips down easily, and it makes a fine match for picnic fare – cold ham, sausage rolls, pâtés and quiches. Beaujolais may have slipped out of fashion since its seventies heyday, but it remains a stalwart crowd-pleaser.

That's the best possible picture of Beaujolais, anyway. The worst manifestation is the dilute Beaujolais Nouveau, enjoyed more for the November ritual of its arrival in the UK soon after vintage rather than the actual pleasure it gives. Poor Beaujolais (and there is plenty of it around) has a smell like nail-varnish remover, a sour-banana flavour and all the concentration of a classroom of ten-year-olds. Happily, there are some effective guidelines for avoiding the worst: side-step Nouveau and basic Beaujolais, and instead go for bottles labelled Beaujolais-Villages, wine made from grapes grown in better sites, or best of all, those produced in ten specific, named villages in the north of the region: St-Amour, Brouilly, Chénas, Chiroubles, Côte de Brouilly, Fleurie, Juliénas, Morgon, Moulin-à-Vent and Regnié. These tend to have more depth of flavour and give a much more satisfying glass of wine, with all the late-summer, squashily ripe, perfumed berry fruit you could possibly want. Georges Duboeuf is the best-known producer, and offers a good introduction to Beaujolais, then try Château Thivin and Louis Jadot's top Beaujolais.

## Matching light and smooth reds with food

Light, smooth reds are a sensible choice if you want to drink red wine on its own, as they are easy to enjoy and have less tannin than other types of red. But these wines go well with food, too, as long as you don't overpower them. Heavy stews, roast lamb and chilli con carne are out; so instead match light reds like Beaujolais, Tarrango and Valpolicella with simple pasta dishes, pizzas and mild cheeses. They have an advantage with creamy sauces, as tannins often clash with cream. That said, fine Pinot Noir goes well with game birds or roast chicken, beef and duck. Choose an older wine with gamier meats. Try red burgundy with rich, creamy and pungent cheeses, too. Very light Pinot, such as that from Alsace, matches fresh salmon well.

# Cabernet Franc

Given the current trend for powerful, rich, ultra-fruity reds, it's not surprising that Cabernet Franc remains relatively unknown. This is a shame, as the grape variety behind the Loire Valley's best reds offers wines with an attractive fresh fragrance, plenty of raspberry character, even a crunchy, pippy quality as if made from just-picked berries. You can almost smell the dew on the currant bushes here, perhaps catch a whiff of freshly mown grass, a slight greenness to the wine. The best, though, have a ripe, concentrated core of red fruit (conversely, poor wines have an underripe, stalky nature). These are wines that seem to come from mid-summer, not late summer, and which should be served, perhaps lightly chilled, with a plate of ham salad or peppery cold beef.

Don't look for the grape variety on the label as you won't find it. Instead, find the location – Chinon and Bourgeuil offer the best. Try Pierre-Jacques Druet, Joguet, Domaine des Roches Neuves. Cabernet Franc is also grown in Bordeaux, where it is the third grape after Cabernet Sauvignon and Merlot in the claret blend, adding fragrance, in particular. Northern Italy also makes Cabernet Franc, but it is on the light, lean, slightly tart side – definitely one for chilling lightly and quaffing on its own. In the newer regions, winemakers have been slow to take up Cabernet Franc, except as a component in a blend, regarding it as a poor cousin to Cabernet Sauvignon. But one or two fine examples do exist, showing that trademark fresh raspberry flavour.

# Other light and smooth reds

**Light Merlot**  The highly fashionable grape variety Merlot makes a range of styles, most of which are medium-bodied (so it's dealt with primarily on pages 94–98). Merlot is usually pretty smooth, fruity and soft, and as such is the perfect blending partner for the more austere and tough Cabernet Sauvignon, in Bordeaux and elsewhere. On its own it ranges from lush, plummy, full and even oaky reds, to refreshingly light, almost grassy, wines. Northern Italy is the source of the most lean and elegant Merlot (or flavourless and insipid, depending on your producer, and to an extent, personal taste).

**Corvina**  Not a well-known grape, but responsible more than any other for the popular Valpolicella of northeast Italy. 'Valpol' is a blend of grapes, but Corvina plays the biggest role, providing red-fruit flavour, and sometimes a hint of marzipan. Don't expect great things from basic Valpolicella, but enjoy the better examples, with their lively, youthful cherry fruit and reasonable depth of flavour.

**Tarrango**  The Tarrango grape gives Australia its very own take on Beaujolais: an extremely soft and easy-drinking red wine with the flavours of banana, cranberry and strawberry. It comes from an Australian cross between the Touriga and Sultana varieties, developed in the 1960s with the express purpose of providing a lighter red than usual in Australia. It needs plenty of heat and ripens well in Australia's warmer vineyards. Brown Brothers is the producer to look out for. Chill Tarrango well before serving and treat it as a simple but refreshing summer red.

**Dornfelder**  Not many people have heard of this grape, but it makes some tempting reds in Germany and even a few wines in England (think aromatic, tangy cherry and strawberry fruit, low tannins, easy to drink). Enjoy these wines young, perhaps a little chilled.

## Storing and serving

Most of the lighter reds need drinking up while they are still young, fresh and vibrant with aromatic red-berry fruit. The richer, smooth reds may be different, though: the most serious Beaujolais (the *crus* described on page 84) will last a few years in bottle and, of course, fine red burgundy is a great 'ager', turning gamey, pungent, even horsey in bottle as it is cellared, often for decades. Serve these bigger soft reds at room temperature, but the lighter ones very slightly chilled to bring out their succulent character.

# shortcuts to success

## FIRST TASTE

• For those unfamiliar with lighter reds, be prepared for a different 'mouth-feel' from these wines. They are not heavy, thick or tannic. Expect a smooth, soft texture and a fresh, tangy finish, even in wines bursting with flavour.

• Before serving, chill these wines lightly to emphasise their succulence.

• The aroma is especially important in these wines. It should be a fresh, berryish perfume, appealing and summery.

## BUYER'S GUIDE

• Avoid the cheapest burgundy as it is likely to be disappointingly thin and jammy. This is one area where the pricier bottles really can be worth it. Not all are good, by any means, but most of the 'bargains' are poor!

• Likewise, steer clear of basic Beaujolais and especially the gimmicky Beaujolais Nouveau. Better Beaujolais is not terrifically expensive. Trade up to bottles labelled Beaujolais-Villages or even better, the individual villages such as Fleurie or Morgon.

• Cabernet Franc is not especially fashionable, but do try the great Loire reds for a refreshing yet satisfying glass of quality lighter red. Look for the appellations Chinon, Bourgeuil and Saumur-Champigny on the label.

## MOVING ON

• Dolcetto tends to give a more serious, soft Italian red than Valpolicella. If you like Italian food and wine, do try Dolcetto from Piedmont with rich pasta bakes.

• Reds from Germany and England will only appeal to the most devoted fan. If you fall into this category, give German and English reds a whirl. Be prepared for some inconsistencies but the occasional fragrant gem.

• Pinot Noir is the best smooth red variety, and it pays to sample plenty of examples from different areas both within and outside Burgundy to appreciate how this grape varies according to its site.

# medium-bodied, soft reds

These are the most versatile reds of all: soft and smooth enough to be thoroughly enjoyable on their own, yet with sufficient depth and concentration to stand up to a wide range of savoury dishes. They clash with very little, can be cracked open on lots of occasions, and rarely offend anyone. The medium-bodied reds are much-loved and appreciated for their easygoing character and their consummate food-friendly quality. Have I made them sound a tad simple? If so, then let me set the record straight. They can be wonderful, beautifully made, perfectly balanced and highly sophisticated. It's just that the smooth reds are not difficult in any way; they are not richly tannic, not tartly crisp, and not packed with heavy wood and spice. They are easy to drink, and hurrah for that.

So it's hardly surprising that wines such as French Merlot, Chianti (made from Sangiovese) and Rioja (Tempranillo) have proved so enduringly popular. In fact, it's difficult to think of many who dislike such wines, so I'm probably preaching to the converted here. But even if you already know and appreciate the medium-bodied reds, there are plenty of tips that can help you both to enjoy them more and to spend your money wisely. They may be easygoing, but there are nonetheless better moments than others for choosing them, perfect dishes for matching with them, and a few wines that are well worth avoiding. Read on…

**APPEARANCE** Bright and lively, often a vivid ruby-red. Not particularly dense or deep, nor pale and weedy-looking. Some wines are a bit richer and more concentrated in colour, edging towards a plummy, youthful, purple-blue hue.

**TEXTURE** Juicy and rounded, with a smooth, succulent finish. These wines should not be too powerful; any heavy oak or spiky tannins will seem out of balance. Then again, they should have some structure and body filling them out. Look for perfect poise, a happy balance between ripe fruit and fresh acidity, with some tannin to firm things up.

# medium-bodied, soft reds

**AROMA** Ripe red fruits galore – plums, strawberries, raspberries, cherries – like a rich summer pudding. Don't expect the dewily fresh, newly squeezed fruit juice of the light reds, however. The perfume of these wines should spell late summer berries, generously fleshy and fulsome. There may be some seductive hints of chocolate, truffles, fresh tobacco, herbs and tea-leaves, with cream and vanilla in oaky examples, more 'green' stalky notes in unripe ones.

**FLAVOUR** Strawberries and plums crop up a lot here, as do creamy, soft depths with hints of vanilla (Rioja) and chocolate (some Merlot). Don't expect the spiciness of the full-bodied reds, but there are some savoury hints – soy, earth, pepper – and perhaps a luxurious finish of creamy coffee which leaves you wanting more. Some of these reds, especially the Italian ones, also have quite pronounced, tangy acidity, too: a twist of sour cherry drops on the finish.

# Merlot

I can't think of anything more fashionable in the world of wine than Merlot. Or to be more specific: Pomerol from Bordeaux, which is mainly Merlot; California Merlot; and at a lower price point, Chilean Merlot. Look around a busy smart restaurant and you can be sure there will be lots of swanky diners plumping for wines made from this grape. They may not know much about it, but they know what's hip and happening, and at the moment that means Merlot. Twenty years ago, it would have been unthinkable. Merlot was considered Cabernet's poor cousin, an inferior blending partner in Bordeaux, and a workhorse grape, turning out less-than-thrilling bottles in other parts of the globe.

So what has happened since? Why has Merlot undergone the sort of image transformation that Travolta was looking for when he met Tarantino? In part, it's due to the fact that many drinkers associate moderate red wine drinking with good health. They are keen to glug on red, believing it is beneficial to their hearts (and there is evidence to back this up), but they don't want a tough, hefty wine like our big reds (see 'Full-bodied Reds' on pages 104–119), or a light, pale red with no guts.

Instead, they want plenty of ripe, juicy fruit – a real red, if you like – but one that tastes soft and easy when young and has few harsh tannins. And one that is widely available and grown all over the world. Merlot fits the bill. One television programme on the health benefits of red wine, broadcast in America a few years ago, is widely considered responsible for giving Merlot's popularity a massive boost.

Then there's the fact that it tastes pretty darn delicious. Merlot has a thoroughly appealing personality. It may not 'wow' you like a glass of blockbuster Aussie Shiraz, but Merlot is beautifully supple, plump and lovable. It has a friendly, plummy flavour, a smooth, rounded texture. It's too complex and serious to be described as 'simple', like, say, Gamay, but nevertheless it is an easy wine to enjoy. Winemakers adore it, too: it grows well in cooler spots than Cabernet and although it can make dilute, bland wine when poorly treated and over-cropped, it often obliges with generously fruity reds.

**FRANCE** I've probably made Merlot sound too jolly and one-dimensional. Anyone coming to the splendid, majestic wines of St-Emilion and Pomerol in Bordeaux, where a high proportion of the blend is Merlot, would beg to disagree. These reds show Merlot at its most serious, concentrated and venerable (these particular examples probably belong in our next chapter, although they are not overtly tannic). In fact, if anyone ever tells you that Merlot counts for little in Bordeaux compared to King Cabernet, a) tell them that it is more widely planted than Cabernet, and b) get them a glass of one of the finest Pomerols and make them drink their words.

Cabernet Sauvignon, Merlot's great blending partner, does indeed hold sway in the Médoc region of France, where its austere cassis and tannin character is fleshed out by the more lush and fruity Merlot component. But on the 'right bank' regions of the Libournais area, and especially its appellations of St-Emilion and Pomerol, Merlot takes over, contributing sixty to one hundred percent of the blend. The rest is usually Cabernet Franc or Cabernet Sauvignon. These wines have a softer, smoother, even more velvety texture than the Cabernet-heavy Médoc wines, and they are unusually rich, inky and intense in ripe fruit flavour and have a extra sheen of oak from new barrel-ageing to round them off and add complexity. They age well for decades, yet they are more approachable when young than other Médoc reds.

## Making the difference

One factor that influences the character of medium-bodied reds is the sort of oak-ageing they receive. Some of the wines described in this chapter are not been aged in oak at all, and have a more immediate, simple, fresh-fruit flavour. This may be true of the southern Italian reds, Portuguese Periquita, some lighter Merlots, and Rioja *sin crianza* ('without oak'), for example. Other wines spend time in barrel, picking up nuances of vanilla, cream and hints of spice and cedar along the way. The majority of Bordeaux reds, California Merlots, and Chianti Classicos are been barrel-aged. Top Pomerols in particular should display a fine, well-balanced oaky layer of complexity. Rioja is matured for years. It is traditionally kept in vanilla-rich American-oak casks to pick up its characteristic mellow, creamy flavour.

## Matching medium-bodied, soft reds with food

Easy! The medium-bodied reds go with a wide range of savoury dishes. They don't have heavy tannins, sharp acidity or excess sugar (or they shouldn't have), which means there is little to clash with the food. Just avoid striking the wrong balance. Don't match medium-bodied reds with very light dishes – leafy salads and grilled white fish are out – as they will overpower the food, and don't crack open a bottle to go with a very hearty stew or heavily spiced meat dish, as the wine won't stand up to it. Otherwise, the choice is yours. Game birds, roast poultry, pork and ham, pasta in meaty sauces, roast vegetables, medium hard cheeses, grilled steaks, hamburgers, pizzas, sausages, shepherd's pie are all good bets. Oh, and Rioja is brilliant with grilled lamb chops and garlic!

The famous *châteaux* of Pomerol command extremely high prices for their wines. A few are clearly overpriced, the wine often bought by fashion victims. Even so, if you ever get a chance to try fine Pomerol from a good vintage, snatch it! Top estates include Pétrus, Le Pin, l'Eglise-Clinet, l'Evangile, Gazin, Lafleur and Trotanoy. It's more tricky to pin down the exact character of St-Emilion as lots of small-scale winemakers work there, producing a range of styles. Some make such small quantities that they are described as *garagistes*, implying that they make their wine in the garage! Ideally, one would repair to this picturesque town and set to work tasting a number *in situ*. You could go for wine from one of the sixty named *crus classés* (classed growths), but don't expect them to be equally good, or anyone feeling particularly wealthy might make straight for the great *châteaux* names, Ausone, Cheval Blanc and Figeac, among others.

Merlot is grown all over the southwest of France and makes up a high proportion of the blend in cheaper reds. Although it is sometimes (and in the case of cheap claret, almost always) dilute and jammy, it can be reasonable value for money, providing you choose carefully. Avoid basic Bordeaux Rouge or cheap claret at all costs and instead seek out wines from the Côtes de Bourg, Côtes de Blaye, Côtes de Francs and Côtes de Castillon for better quality. I can't tell you exactly how much Merlot will be in the blend for each wine, but a youngish bottle that is relatively soft and easygoing, with juicy, red-berry character, is likely to contain a high proportion. Sometimes the back label will let you know. If you're on a budget, try the wines of a wider area, such as Buzet, Marmandais, Duras and Bergerac, too, as they are made from Bordeaux varieties, often leaning heavily towards Merlot in the blend.

Don't miss the *Vin de Pays d'Oc* Merlot from the deep south of France, either. It may not set the world on fire with its depth and complexity, but this is usually modern, fruit-driven, gluggable stuff at a decent price and it will appeal to modern wine-drinkers.

**REST OF EUROPE**  Northern Italy makes a lighter, more refreshing style of Merlot that really belongs in the previous section, 'Light and Smooth Reds' (see pages 78–89). A few quite different and much more serious wines are produced in central Italy, especially Tuscany, where Merlot is one of the grapes used for the much-admired 'Super-Tuscans': a newish breed made with international grapes as well as local ones. Expect quite chunky, oaky Merlot, or delicious blends with Cabernet or with local grape Sangiovese. Prices are high, and results a bit erratic, but sometimes the Super-Tuscans do shine, especially those from top wineries Avignonesi, Castello di Brolio, Castello di Fonterutoli, Ornellaia and Luce. A few intensely plummy, fairly weighty Merlots are being made in Sicily by progressive wineries; these are reliable, good value wines in the non-European, fruit-driven style.

Spanish reds are mainly made from Tempranillo, but Cabernet has gradually crept into more and more bottles, and so, to a lesser degree, has Merlot. The Navarra region, a neighbour of Rioja in northwest Spain, has a progressive, modern wine industry, so it is not surprising to see Merlot pop up there. Navarran Merlots are appealingly ripe and well-balanced, and usually a little oaky. Try Palacio de la Vega or Castillo de Montjardin. Find Merlot in Penedés (another go-ahead, fashion-conscious region), Somontano, and even in the blend for one of Spain's most acclaimed reds, Vega Sicilia from the Ribera del Duero region.

In fact, Merlot is stretching its trendy tendrils into almost every winemaking country these days. Austria produces some decent, chunky Bordeaux blends, or mixes of Bordeaux grapes with its own varieties, although these bottles are a rare find abroad. Greece has a few Merlot plantings, and Eastern Europe still turns out some good-value bottles, although these have been rather trumped by non-European cheapies in recent years. Still, some Bulgarian Merlot impresses for its clean, bright fruit and decent oak. It's a shame that Bulgaria's wine industry isn't in better shape, as quality is currently unreliable. If you find a good one, congratulate yourself, as you've probably got a bargain. Domaine Boyar's Blueridge label is a fairly safe bet.

**REST OF THE WORLD** Californians have taken Merlot to their hearts – literally, they hope, as they sip the stuff and wait to live that bit longer – and there's plenty around from the West Coast. The worst can be too sweetly ripe, with unsubtle oak and a confected finish, but the best are superb. Concentrated, even chunky wines, packed with plum, cherry and rich chocolate, are made in Napa Valley, and other areas. Blends of Bordeaux grapes can be serious too, although someone has coined the rather horrible name 'Meritage' to label them. There is some evidence that the Merlot craze is wearing off a bit as punters get fed up with the poor, cheap wines. There will always be Merlot mania to some degree on the West Coast, however – let's hope only the best wines survive any future backlash. Try Duckhorn, Beringer, Newton and Shafer wines. And give Washington State Merlot a whirl, too; it may not be too familiar, but can be bright and lively, as can Long Island's take on this grape.

Australia has surprisingly few Merlots, despite its reputation as a red-wine producer extraordinaire. The Aussies have preferred to concentrate on grapes which flourish in their very warm vineyards, hence loads of Cabernet and Shiraz, but less Merlot. More have appeared in the last year or two, and same are impressively fruity. In New Zealand, Merlot is extremely promising, particularly in the relatively warm Hawke's Bay region of the country. As the Kiwis get to grips more firmly with red wines, we can expect greater things from their Merlot. Waiheke Island, a hot spot out in Auckland Harbour, is another place excelling with reds, and Bordeaux-style blends in particular. Successful wineries include Esk Valley, Sileni, Goldwater and Stonyridge. South Africa is another country that is starting prove it can shine with Merlot, in this case, some remarkably ripe, dark wines, particularly from Stellenbosch, Paarl and Malmesbury regions. Spice Route, Plaisir de Merle, De Toren and Warwick all make admirable Merlots or Merlot blends.

A few promising Merlots are emerging from Argentina, but for now the Argentinian Malbecs and Syrahs are more impressive. Which leaves us with Chile and some of the best-value reds in the world. Chilean Merlot is immediately likeable, its delicious fresh fruit rounded out by a richer chocolate/mocha, even smoky note. Don't expect anything like the sophistication of top Bordeaux. These are wines for everyday drinking – okay, more like Saturday night quaffing. Think medium-bodied, medium price. They are very reliable and justly popular. Oddly, a proportion of Chilean 'Merlot' was recently found to be another grape entirely, Carmenère, which has become muddled up in the vineyards. Carmenère is now being labelled as such, and luckily turns out to make rather good red in its own right, with a slightly more pronounced savoury/soy character. Try both and see if you can tell them apart. Some of the best Chilean Merlot/Merlot blends are made by Viña Carmen, Casa Lapostolle and Villard wineries.

# Other medium-bodied, soft reds

**Sangiovese**  Sangiovese means 'blood of Jove' which doesn't sound especially tempting, somehow. Never mind; it's one of Italy's premium grapes and the mainstay of Tuscan reds, where it forms the base for the world-famous and perennially popular Chianti. Other grapes are used in the Chianti blend, but Sangiovese is the principal variety, while Brunello di Montalcino, another great Tuscan classic, is made solely from it.

This vine ripens slowly, and that can cause problems, namely stalky green wine from grapes that haven't had enough sun. There used to be plenty of poor Chianti around that displayed exactly such a fault, but thankfully the problem is more firmly under control these days. In fact, cast all memories of cheap seventies' raffia flasks from your mind. Chianti, and particularly Chianti Classico, from the heart of the region, is pretty good stuff, aromatic with strawberries, tea-leaves and fresh cigars, and with that tangy twist of slightly sour cherries to give it a fresh lift and makes it so food-friendly.

The most exciting wines, though, are the riper, beefier, heartier Chiantis – still refreshing and smooth, but without a trace of weediness. Blends with Merlot (the dynamic new breed of 'Super-Tuscan' reds, see page 97) are interesting and worthwhile, too. For the best of Sangiovese, go for Isole e Olena, Monte Vertine, Querciabella, Gaja and Frescobaldi. Little is made outside Italy, although the Californians show the most interest and produce one or two excellent examples, such as Seghesio's blend of Sangiovese and Cabernet, and straight varietal wines from Flora Springs and Il Podere dell' Olivos.

**Tempranillo**  As Sangiovese is the great grape of Italy's most famous red wine, so Tempranillo is the main variety behind Spain's most lauded wine, Rioja. The Rioja region of northwest Spain has been making distinctive, oak-aged reds for over a century. Don't make the mistake of thinking red Rioja is big, heavy and tannic. It is mellow, smooth, aged at the *bodega* (winery) in cask and then bottled so that it's ready to drink on release. The typical flavours are cream and vanilla (from long ageing in American oak, which gives more of this character than French oak) and aromatic, sweetly ripe strawberry fruit. Garnacha plays an important part in some blends, and smaller amounts of the Spanish grapes Graciano (which gives structure and tannin) and Mazuelo (aka Carignan, for colour and body) are often used. In a few blends Cabernet Sauvignon has been successfully brought in, though these wines are officially just 'experiments'.

There are several different categories of red Rioja, according to the length of oak-ageing. A few cheaper, less interesting wines will be young (*joven*), unoaked (*sin crianza*) or very lightly oaked (*semi-crianza*), but all serious, traditional Rioja sees the inside of an oak barrel for a significant period of time. The word *crianza* on a label indicates a year in oak, and further bottle-age before release; a *reserva* requires three years' ageing, at least one of which must be in cask and another in bottle; and *gran reserva* means five years' maturation, at least two in bottle and two in cask. Each of these last three groups is worthwhile. *Crianza* is the liveliest of the trio, with more sprightly fresh, red-berry fruit; *reserva* starts to show velvety smoothness and mellow flavours; while *gran reserva* should be a wine of great maturity, depth and roundness.

Variations on the theme include those Cabernet blends, wines with more rich, tannic characteristics, and wines aged in French oak, but to me and many other fans, red Rioja is all about that soft, creamy oak and bags of strawberry aroma and flavour. That means American oak, long ageing and the Sangiovese grape. But to make sure you get a bottle you like, it pays to learn the house style of several different *bodegas*, and watch out for those categories of ageing described on the label. The best *bodegas* include El Coto, Marqués de Griñón, López de Heredia, Martínez-Bujanda, Montecillo, Muga, Marqués de Murrieta, Palacio, La Rioja Alta, Marqués de Riscal and Bodegas Roda. Great recent vintages are 2001, 1999, 1996, 1995, 1994, and 1990.

## Dolcetto and Barbera

These are two grapes grown in Piedmont, northern Italy, that live in the shadow of the more famous local grape Nebbiolo, and are not hugely well-known outside Italy. They are well worth seeking out. Both provide better-than-average, highly food-friendly wine and rarely disappoint.

Dolcetto (the 'little sweet one') makes soft wines with a succulent, red-cherry flavour and plenty of acidity – even a slightly sour twist on the end. This helps the wine to cut through fatty food, and Dolcetto is a star turn with rich, meaty pasta sauces or cheesy pasta bakes. It has been described as the Gamay (Beaujolais grape) of northern Italy, although I tend to think it is better than that, and can make some excellent, intensely fruity wines, some of which descend into delicious chocolatey depths. Top labels are Domenico Clerico, Bruno Giacosa, Mascarello and Voerzio.

There is less argument today about the sophistication of premium Barbera, plummy and fresh yet ripe and satisfying. Those who find Nebbiolo, the grape behind Barolo and Barbaresco (see page 116), too much like hard work, should go for Barbera. It used to be seen as the source of everyday, straightforward reds, but in the last fifteen years or so some producers (many the same as those named above for Nebbiolo) have taken it more seriously, planting it in better sites, cutting back on the fruit yields, using fine oak barrels to age it. Some of the resulting wines have shown Barbera make the leap to a first-rate red.

## Nero d'Avola, Primitivo, Negroamaro and Montepulciano

Four more Italian grapes (this country is clearly a maestro when it comes to medium-bodied reds). The first three hail from much further south, where they are the local varieties behind many of Italy's new-wave, inexpensive reds.

Puglia is the most important region for decent wines made from this grape – expect soft, moreish, plummy reds, and plain chocolate hints from Negroamaro – though you might try the appellation of Salice Salentino, too. Primitivo is thought to be the same grape as Zinfandel, which makes big, gutsy reds in California (see page 117). Montepulciano makes lots of agreeably fresh and easy-drinking red in central and southeast Italy.

## Periquita

Portugal is enjoying a new wave of popularity for its cheap, but pleasant reds from the central regions of the country. These are smooth and juicy with cherry, strawberry and red plum flavours although they need drinking up while they are young. Periquita is the variety behind many of these wines, which are a sensible, low-budget choice for pleasing a crowd at a party. Supermarkets usually stock fair Portuguese reds made from Periquita at low prices.

## Cinsault

I can't pretend to be a big fan of Cinsault, which often makes uninspiring reds in southern France and rather rough ones in South Africa (where it is spelt Cinsaut). But it has its fans, particularly for the occasional new-wave wines that have been made from the grapes of low-yielding old vines.

## Bonarda

Argentinian softie, making very moreish (at best), very smooth, inexpensive reds that taste of squashy ripe cherries and cassis. Quality is a bit patchy and some wines are on the decidedly light side.

## Storing and serving

The medium reds should not be kept for many years unless they are the striking, concentrated, expensive top wines of Bordeaux, California and Italy. These majestic bottles can be cellared for many years and become more drinkable, softer and more mellow with time. But no-nonsense, everyday softies should be enjoyed within one year of purchase or they will start to lose their vibrant-berry, fruit flavour. Red Rioja is aged in barrel, then in the bottle at the *bodega* (winery), and is released ready to drink. Do not age it for years or it might start to taste tired. Serve all the wines described in this chapter at room temperature, in big wine glasses so you can swirl the liquid around and release those lovely fruity aromas.

# shortcuts to success

## FIRST TASTE

• Red fruits rule here! Expect masses of strawberry, cherry, red plums. If your medium red lacks fruity character, there's something wrong with it.

• The body and structure should be well-balanced – neither too light and jammy, nor too heavy and tannic. These reds are meant to be rounded, silky and relatively easy to drink when young.

• Beware the green, stalky medium red. This means the grapes were not ready when they were picked. Smooth, juicy reds cannot be made from underripe grapes. Avoid that label in the future.

• Look out for chocolatey notes in many of these wines. They are not just about red fruit, but often about a choccy, creamy, vanilla roundness, too.

• And many have a tangy finish, ending on a mouth-watering note, or even a slightly tart note. This is especially true of the medium-bodied Italian reds, and it means the wines seem to cut through rich food well.

# BUYER'S GUIDE

• The top Merlot-rich wines from Bordeaux (St-Emilion, Pomerol) and the finest California Merlots and Merlot/Cabernets are extremely expensive. Some of them are magnificent, the apogee of this style, but you will rarely find a bargain. These are cult wines.

• But don't go to the other extreme and buy the very cheapest claret (red Bordeaux). This is often Merlot at its most mundane and dilute. Try something in between; perhaps spend a little more on a bottle to sample decent Bordeaux. Or go for Vin de Pays d'Oc Merlot for a reliable cheapie.

• Likewise, avoid basic inexpensive California Merlot, which can be sweetish, over-oaky and unsubtle.

• Chilean Merlot is great value for money: ultra-fruity, easy-drinking, soft and friendly stuff. It's consistent, too, and has bags of plummy flavour and chocolate. Don't miss it.

• South Africa is making some of the most impressive Merlot and Merlot blends for a fair price. Snap up South African Merlot before the Cape starts to charge more for such good wine.

• Great everyday gluggers include wines from Puglia in southern Italy and Periquita in Portugal, providing red berries, medium body and a soft texture.

# MOVING ON

• Try Merlot from unusual sources – Austria, Sicily or New Zealand, for example – to see how its place of origin shapes its character. This is a well-travelled grape that is made all over the winemaking world.

• Sample the range of styles this grape makes, from light, refreshing northern Italian Merlots, to fruit-driven, warm-climate bottles, to the chunkier, more serious Bordeaux wines.

• Dolcetto and Barbera are must-haves from Italy: two grape varieties from Piedmont which have a wonderful cherry and plum flavour and are increasingly taken seriously by thoughtful winemakers in the region. If you like the better-known Chianti, then give these wines a go.

• Chianti Classico and Rioja reserva are two extremely food-friendly types of red (the first from Tuscany, the second from northern Spain). Chianti and Rioja are both great choices when dining, as they go with a wide range of foods. They are often reasonably priced, too.

• Rioja fans, be aware that there are different types of red Rioja according to the amount of time matured in oak; also some wines are aged in French oak, not traditional American casks, and some are made with the addition of Cabernet. Not all Rioja tastes the same!

# full-bodied reds

The full-bodied reds are not for the faint-hearted. They fill your mouth with rich fruit and tannin, spice and oak, and the flavours and textures seem to linger long after they have been swallowed. Younger wines tend to be chewier and firmer, older ones are gentler and more mellow while retaining concentrated fruit and intensity. Poor ones are either too dilute and simply jammy or they are unbalanced – too much oak, too much tannin, too much sweetly ripe, 'in-yer-face' cassis flavour – and taste overwhelming. Watch out for wines that impress you on first taste, but which you wouldn't drink in any quantity. These are often referred to as 'show wines'; they win awards for their extra clout, but don't always make for enjoyable drinking.

That said, if you generally prefer lighter reds, think twice before writing off richer, more full-bodied wines. Like so many styles, but perhaps even more so in this case, they should be cracked open at exactly the right moment to be appreciated fully, not brought out on every occasion. For example, blockbuster reds do not make great party wines. They are neither soft nor mellow enough to slip down without food; that big-framed tannic structure may only make sense with a forkful of a rare steak. Similarly, they do not suit hot weather, or outdoor wining and dining. Although they might match a barbecued meat fest, their high alcohol and richness can be a quick route to a headache. Stick to medium or light styles of red on a picnic or at a party.

So, bring out the heavyweights only to partner robust winter dishes: peppery stews, roast red meats, fine cheeseboards and rich vegetarian bakes. Used carefully, these can be the ultimate comfort wines: soothing, heart-warming, contentment-enducing. Some of them age well, too, so cellar-owners should take careful note of what follows. The big reds are like all hefty and daunting things in life: potentially overwhelming but wonderful when handled correctly.

## APPEARANCE
Dark red, ranging from a port-like, concentrated garnet to brighter, richly purple and even damson-black. Most look intense, dense in colour if you hold a glassful up to the light. Younger wines tend to be a more bluey-purple; older ones are mahogany-brown.

## TEXTURE
Tannin – the substance that gives wine a lot of rich body and structure, and an almost 'chewy' mouth feel, like sucking on a wooden pencil – can feature heavily here, especially in younger bottles. Other wines have a more rounded quality, but retain that rich weightiness in the mouth.

# full-bodied reds

**AROMA**  The fruit aromas tend to be blackcurrant and blackberry, sometimes very pungent, like a whiff of crème de cassis. Hints of toffee, spice, black pepper, eucalyptus, treacle, tar, liquorice and mint sometimes feature. Very oaky wines have a strong vanilla character, even sawdust-like on the nose.

**FLAVOUR**  Fruit flavours include an intense blackcurrant akin to black fruit gums – also briar fruits, brambles, and raspberries in certain wines. Look out, too, for a twist of spice (cloves, cinnamon) and especially black pepper on the finish, chocolate, spicy vanillins and chewy tannins, too. Older wines have a leather or suede character.

# Cabernet Sauvignon

Cabernet is often referred to as the 'king' of red grapes. Why? It's astonishingly popular among consumers and winemakers, it is grown all over the world and, in most places, it makes at least good, and often great, wine. In terms of reliability it reigns supreme – most Cabernet is palatable and complete duds are relatively rare. It often makes firm and full-bodied reds capable of long ageing, it takes well to maturation in French-oak barrels, picking up aromatic hints of cedar and vanilla, and it blends well with other varieties, particularly Merlot and Shiraz. No wonder it is often described in the same breath as Chardonnay in terms of popularity. This is one red grape with which winemakers aspire to make their greatest wines.

The main attributes of top Cabernet are its wonderfully concentrated cassis character, its firm structure and effortless ageing ability. Look out for the former when you sip this wine. A good example will not only ooze blackcurrant but may well have complex undertones of mint, plain chocolate, lead pencil, cedar and fresh cigars. It may all sound a bit fanciful, but this is one deep and meaningful grape, and tasters find all sorts of nuances in there. With age (in the wine, not the taster) they spot leather, game, marmite, earth... Let your inner poet go wild when you describe Cabernet to yourself. That rich, often tannic structure is derived from the fact that the Cabernet vine forms thick-skinned, small-berried grapes with a high proportion of skin and pips compared to the amount of juice they contain. This gives wine with plenty of rich, purple colour and high levels of tannin. It also explains the reason why certain wines age well, their tannins softening over time. Blending Cabernet with other fleshier grapes – Merlot, for example – fills out this somewhat tough flavour with some more easily approachable fruitiness.

**FRANCE**  Red Bordeaux, or claret, may be disappointing at the cheaper end of the market, but few would dispute the fact that top examples remain some of the most serious and exciting red wines in the world. Although plantings of Merlot exceed Cabernet in Bordeaux, it can be argued that the latter rules in the region. Red Bordeaux still spells Cabernet for most drinkers – Cabernet filled out by Merlot and Cabernet

Franc in the blend, but essentially Cabernet in all its venerable, aromatic, cassis-drenched glory, almost sweetly ripe, dry on the finish, the ripe fruit held up by a firm structure of tannins.

The world of wine is never straightforward. In truth, a lot of inexpensive clarets rely on Merlot more heavily; the worst tend towards jammy, dilute dross, while in the great Merlot estates of St-Emilion and Pomerol (see pages 94–97), Cabernet plays a very minor role in the blend. But in the Médoc, on the left bank of the Gironde, close to the Atlantic and protected by the forests of Les Landes, Cabernet is the main player in some of the most sought-after and well-loved wines of all – those from the villages of the Haut-Médoc: Margaux, St-Julien, Pauillac and St-Estèphe. Here the vines grow in well-drained, gravel soils near to the Gironde estuary. Some of the glitteringly famous chateaux of Haut-Médoc are Château Margaux (Margaux); Léoville-Barton, Gruaud-Larose (St-Julien), Latour, Lafite, Mouton-Rothschild (Pauillac) and Cos d'Estournel (St-Estèphe). Expect very high prices indeed for these much sought-after wines.

Another part of the region where Cabernet is dominant is the Graves, closer to the city of Bordeaux. The best wines come from the Pessac-Léognan area of Graves, and include the first-growth Haut-Brion. First growth? The Bordeaux classification system is something that all traditional wine buffs make an effort to master, even though it sometimes seems ludicrously old-fashioned and out of touch. It works on a pyramid structure with five tiers of *crus classés* (classed growths). The most important summary of rankings was made in 1855. (See what I mean about outmoded?) Today there is much controversy over which *châteaux* deserve demotion and promotion. For example, some fifth-growth *châteaux*, such as Lynch-Bages and Grand-Puy-Lacoste, make superb wines that belie their relatively low ranking. Make your own mind up by trying as many as possible (though let's hope you are being treated, as prices for top clarets are, of course, sky-high). Those who are impressed by famous classed-growth labels should note that ninety percent of wine made in the commune of Pauillac is classed-growth and its *châteaux* Latour, Lafite and Mouton-Rothschild are all first growths. It should be said that some of these wines are truly remarkable in terms of complexity, depth of flavour, fine balance and longevity. Then again, some wonder what all the fuss is about. The only answer is to try out fine claret and see what you think.

For those of us who haven't won the lottery, the Médoc region of Bordeaux also produces plenty of generic red wine for a much lower outlay. Here's a useful hint: try wines labelled 'Crus Bourgeois', the category just below classed growth. Within this group, the many *châteaux* are well worth a whirl and often offer some fine drinking at a reasonable price. Or try the 'second wines' of the great *châteaux*, made either from rejected blends of the top houses or from the fruit of young, up-and-coming vines. Taste Les Forts de Latour or Pavillon Rouge from Château Margaux, among others – not exactly cheap, but cheaper. When buying both these good-value wines and the classed growths, it's important to choose wine from a decent vintage: these not only taste better when young, they age better, too. Recent fine vintages include 2000, 1997 (for earlier drinking), 1995, 1990, 1989 and 1988. For more on the slightly lighter generic clarets and Merlot-heavy blends from the region, see the section on 'Medium-bodied, Soft Reds' (pages 90–103).

## Making the difference

The full-bodied, almost mouth-coating texture of the world's biggest reds comes from tannin, which is a substance found in the skins, pips and stalks of grapes. Tannins are a group of complex organic substances also found in bark and other fruits. Tannin from pips is bitter, so canny winemakers take care to avoid crushing the seeds. Some avoid using stems in the mix as well, although others think they benefit the finished wine. The skins provide more benevolent tannins and plenty of colour, too. Powerful reds are made from small berries with thick skins so their concentration of tannin and colour is higher than average. The grapes must be ripe, or a nasty, furry, green tannic character is the result. Extra tannin is added when a wine is aged in new-oak barrels, which leach some of their wood character into the wine.

Bergerac makes a few wines from the Cabernet grape that are relatively full-bodied, but in general they are softer than in Bordeaux's most famous areas. Some rich Cabernets and Cabernet blends can be found in the wider southwest of France, including thick, ripe modern wines from the Languedoc. Generally speaking, these tend to lack the subtlety and ageing potential of the top clarets, and have a rather 'New World' sunny, blackcurrant flavour, but they can be good value if you want a modern, fruit-driven wine.

**REST OF EUROPE**  Spain has proved it can make some impressive Cabernet, mainly in Penedès (thank you, Miguel Torres and Jean León, who pioneered international grapes here), although plenty of other regions are now throwing Cabernet into the blend. In Rioja and Ribera del Duero, progressive winemakers blend it with the main variety Tempranillo for some successful, ripe reds, while Navarra makes some fruity, straightforward, single-varietal Cabs. Ribera's Vega Sicilia makes one of the most famous Spanish reds of all: a long-lived blend of Tempranillo, Cabernet, Merlot and Malbec.

It's a similar story in Italy, where winemakers tend to use Cabernet to make interesting, premium blends with Merlot or the Tuscan grape, Sangiovese. It's becoming increasingly important in central Italy, where many serious, concentrated reds are based on Cabernet. This means the wines fall foul of the local regulations (Cabernet isn't allowed) and can't attain normal DOCG status. These wild-card wines are known as 'Super-Tuscans' and are much admired by collectors of fine Italian reds. The most famous are made by the Antinori winery.

Eastern Europe, and particularly Bulgaria, is known for cheap-and-cheerful Cabernet. No longer as popular an everyday glugger as it once was, Bulgarian Cabernet can still be pleasant, with clean cassis fruit, a rounded texture and some creamy oak in most examples. These wines are a bit 'mass-market', however, fairly boring,

and not quite as rich as one might hope for. Still, they are doggedly cheap. Domaine Boyar is the name to go for if you want to try a Bulgarian Cabernet.

Finally, Austria is perhaps a surprising source of decent Cabernet, usually in the form of blends with Merlot and sometimes local Austrian grapes. The Burgenland region makes the majority of worthwhile examples.

**REST OF THE WORLD**  In the newer wine-producing regions, more premium wines are made from Cabernet than from any other grape. Many winemakers here aspire to a 'flagship' wine that is made from pure Cabernet or, more usually, a classic Bordeaux blend. This is a variety that travels well, producing fine wine in many sites, providing there is enough heat for it to ripen sufficiently, as this is a slow developer, and as long as soils don't get too wet. It generally obliges, coming up with that signature cassis in warm southern hemisphere countries, usually a particularly ripe and juicy note, and plenty of colour and body.

Of course, there are exceptions and those pursuing warm-climate Cabernet should be aware that blandness can be a problem. Simple, fruity, one-dimensional wines are all very well if you don't give a hoot for the fact that this grape is capable of so much more. Cabernet is now so overwhelmingly popular that some wineries simply churn it out as a cheap, commercial wine because putting this grape on a label means it will sell. It's easy to get bored with these wines, and inevitably some wise drinkers will switch to more exciting, if lesser-known varieties. So watch out – reasonably palatable just isn't good enough from this great grape variety.

Argentina has been guilty of making Cabernets like this for the past few years and although a few decent examples are made here, there are more exciting Argentinian reds to be had from the Malbec and Syrah grapes (see pages 115–116). Neighbouring

Chile is more exciting when it comes to Cabernet. A fine, classic Chilean Cabernet strikes a memorably pure, clear, bright blackcurrant note – like eating a big spoonful of shiny fruit from a baked currant pie. Take into account the low prices of many bottles and it's easy to see why the Chilean style is immensely popular. Rapel is one region to look out for, and some of the top labels from Chile are made by Errázuriz, Santa Rita and Santa Carolina. The mid-price bracket is where it excels; cheapies can be a bit mundane, and Chile has yet to prove it can make truly great, top-rank Cabernet and Cabernet blends in significant numbers.

Further north, California is the source of some monster Cabernets – monster in the sense of big, brooding, ultra-concentrated wines with loads of extract and decades of life ahead of them. These are wines to take seriously; the top ones can rival Bordeaux in terms of complexity and longevity, although it can be argued that they are a little less subtle, and major in thick, rich fruit and vanilla rather than anything else. Unsurprisingly, they are expensive and are often snapped up by rich American collectors, who squirrel them away in cellars for years. The best come from the Napa Valley, Sonoma and some sites south of San Francisco Bay; coolish hillside sites producing the most interesting wines. Watch out for some unbalanced, heavily alcoholic numbers, although thankfully these have diminished in recent years and quality seems to be on the up. Producers to go for include Beringer, Caymus, Hess Collection, Mondavi, Opus One, Joseph Phelps and Screaming Eagle (though strictly for millionnaires). Try Washington State's Cabernet, too – it's beginning to show great promise, with wines tasting intensely fruity.

Australia's best reds are made from Shiraz – a personal view, but there you go. Still, its Cabernet comes a close second. Basic cheap blends of Cabernet and Shiraz can be a bit boring and bland, but more serious examples – you have to spend more – tend to be flavour-packed and chunky. Cabernet on its own varies in character from region to region, which will surprise those who think all Aussie wine tastes the same! Coonawarra is an area well worth exploring, its famous 'terra rossa' iron-rich soils providing exciting, elegant wines which are nonetheless packed with fruit and firm structure. Padthaway, Clare Valley and McLaren Vale give different interpretations; look out for notes of chocolate, eucalyptus, blackberry and wine gums, and make up your own mind about which regional style you prefer. Margaret River, south of Perth in the west, makes particularly compelling, subtle-yet-powerful Cabernet and Cabernet blends. Top producers from across the country include Penfolds, Cullen, Leeuwin Estate, Chapel Hill and Yalumba.

Look out, too, for some excellent, gutsy wines from South Africa. A few years ago, Cape Cabernet and Cabernet blends looked much less promising as many vineyards were diseased. Dull, fruitless, tired wines were all too often the experience. Now, virus-free clones have matured and, in general, South African winemaking has wised up to overseas competition and started to compete more cleverly. The future looks bright. The warm Stellenbosch region is clearly the best for Cabernet, with Paarl vineyards a close second. Top labels include Clos Malverne, Vergelegen, De Toren, De Trafford, Grangehurst, Plaisir de Merle and Rustenberg.

That covers all the major Cabernet-producing countries, but Cabernet hunters should look out for the occasional gem from New Zealand – Bordeaux-style blends of Cabernet and Merlot, sometimes with Cabernet Franc and Malbec, from the Hawke's Bay region of the North Island is currently the most successful formula. And then there's the Lebanon, where one winery, Château Musar, puts out a blend of Cabernet with the lesser-known Cinsault grape which has become a rich, leathery, spicy cult red. A must if you are exploring this variety – although not everyone sings its praises.

# Syrah/Shiraz

Syrah and Shiraz are one and the same grape variety – Syrah is the French name, and Shiraz is the name given to it in Australia, South Africa and other parts of the world. This grape variety is a must if you want to experience the richer, darker side of red wine. Not all Syrahs/Shirazes (or blends that incorporate it) will be satisfyingly full-on, so watch out for some weedy, jammy cheapies, but in the main, this is one of the grapes to go for if you want a heavyweight. It doesn't often deliver fresh, fruity flavours, however.

Syrah/Shiraz can be lots of things, but it isn't in the 'fruit salad' school of wine. It's hard to swirl a glass of the stuff and find raspberries, strawberries, plums and cassis, as you will with many red grapes. Instead, potent, wilder aromas assail the nostrils – of spice, black pepper, toffee, cream, herbs, smoke, citrus peel, leather – and the taste is similar. Sure, there's a rich blackberry/ blackcurrant element in certain, especially non-European Shirazes, but those unusual characteristics are what stand out, and what make this grape so misunderstood and often underrated. It was often used as a 'workhorse', churning out cheap and rough reds, especially in Australia, until the modern era kicked in and winemakers started making first-rate, premium reds from it. Those who liked powerful, robust wines loved Shiraz, and so a modern classic was born.

Of course, as Syrah, this grape was always much appreciated. The Rhône Valley is renowned for its gutsy, concentrated, sun-baked reds, and Syrah has always played a major part in these. This variety's popularity is set to grow as more winemakers around the world take it on and come up with startlingly good results. Still, for now it remains less well-known than Cabernet, Merlot and Pinot Noir. So, if you haven't discovered Shiraz/Syrah yet, make a point of doing so now. Note it is made in the warmer parts of the winemaking globe, where the hot sun coaxes the grapes into full ripeness.

**FRANCE** The huge, smouldering reds of the northern Rhône Valley are made almost entirely from Syrah. This is a sunny area that starts at Vienne, with the appellation of Côte-Rôtie ('roasted slope'), and runs southwards to St-Péray, near the town of Valence. The wines are dense, intense, super-concentrated with a twist of black pepper and a rich, rounded texture. Some have a sprinkling of white Viognier grapes in the blend, which gives the liquid a fragant lift. Côte-Rôtie's winemakers are arguably the greatest in the south, making brooding monsters packed with black fruit and spice, but don't pass up the chance for a decent bottle from the appellations of Crozes-Hermitage, Hermitage, St-Joseph and Cornas, either. Names such as Chapoutier, Chave, Graillot, Delas, Guigal, Paul Jaboulet and Noël Verset are all worth exploring. The best wines are thoroughly age-worthy, their heavy structure softening and loosening up over time.

The southern section of the Rhône begins below Montélimar and is a hot, arid place where rich, headily alcoholic reds are the norm. The most famous wine of the region is the purple-hued, heavyweight Châteauneuf-du-Pape, made from a heady mix of up to thirteen different grape varieties, mainly Grenache (see below) but also Syrah and Mourvèdre. Vineyards contain big flat stones which retain the heat of the sun well into the evening. Other southern Rhône reds produced from a similar blend include Gigondas, Lirac and Vacqueyras. Again, the top wines should mature well for years. Further down the prestige ladder come sixteen named Côtes du Rhône-Villages (including Cairanne, Rasteau and Beaumes-de-Venise), then generic Côtes du Rhône-Villages, which are often good value for money, and below that the cheapish Côtes du Rhône reds, which can occasionally please

## Matching full-bodied reds with food

Don't serve these wines on their own as they are too heavy, and don't even think about matching them with light salads, fish or seafood (salted cod is the only exception), cold chicken, mild cheeses… the wines will walk all over the food and you will hardly taste your dinner. Instead, find a dish that is hearty enough to match your blockbuster wine. Roast red meats, rich stews, peppery steaks, full-flavoured cheeses and hot cheesy bakes are all good candidates. More specifically, match decent Médoc with roast lamb (the mint and blackcurrant of Cabernet complement lamb perfectly), Argentinian Malbec with steak (a modern classic in Buenos Aires), Shiraz/Syrah with game birds or beef casseroles, Barolo and Amarone with fine hard cheeses, Zinfandel with classic Christmas turkey and trimmings, and Pinotage with char-grilled barbecued meats.

## Storing and serving

Avoid committing infanticide! Too many drinkers buy a full-bodied red and crack it open when it is far too young, ending up with a tough, chewy wine in their glass instead of a mature, mellow mouthful. Beware youthful claret, Barolo and Barbaresco, top Rhône reds and the most serious Australian reds in particular. They will age well for years, if not decades. Store them on their sides in a cool, dark place and leave them well alone! Cheaper wines tend to be made for earlier drinking: within a year or two of purchase. Serve them at room temperature and decant any very heavy reds, just like port, to open up their aroma, soften their texture and possibly remove any solid dregs that lurk at the bottom of the bottle.

but are often basic and a bit dilute. Château de Beaucastel, Château Rayas and Domaine du Vieux Télégraphe are all top labels. In the south of France, Syrah is often used in blends or on its own to make modern, flavoursome reds with a black-wine-gum flavour – these will appeal to lovers of non-European Shiraz and Cabernet.

**AUSTRALIA** This is the country that relied on Shiraz (as they call it) as a trusty servant for over a century, turning out fortified wine and basic 'dry reds' from it until finally realising it could (and should) be taken far more seriously. Now it is one of Australia's trump cards, producing some of its most awesome wines, much of it from ancient vines which yield small harvests of wonderfully concentrated grapes. The result is big, powerful, mouth-filling red, heavy on the black-fruit pastilles, chewy and lingering, smooth and often velvety in its flavour – the gentle giants of the red-wine world. Australian Shiraz is reliable, too – you will rarely encounter a complete horror, so if you like this style of wine, you are on to a good thing. Blends of Shiraz with Cabernet produce some rather mundane, soft reds, but other compellingly rich bins.

The most famous Aussie Shiraz is Penfolds' Grange. It's an amazingly long-lived, intense red made mainly from fruit grown in the hot Barossa Valley, South Australia, one of the best sources of Shiraz in the country. Grange is not cheap, to put it mildly. In the Hunter Valley, New South Wales, Shiraz has a reputation for being leathery and with an aroma of 'sweaty saddles', but the vaguely grubby styles of the past have made way for cleaner, fruitier wines. McLaren Vale Shiraz can be honest, big, chocolatey stuff, Victoria makes peppery, perfumed variants, and Western Australia makes cassis-laden wines with subtle nuances of eucalyptus and mint. Look out for these and other regional characteristics. Which names should you watch for? Top labels include Penfolds, Hardy's top wines, Peter Lehmann, Rothbury, Henschke, Jasper Hill, Charles Melton, Mount Langi Ghiran, Tatachilla, Yalumba and Jim Barry, but cheaper own-label brands can be tasty, too.

**REST OF THE WORLD** This is currently a fashionable variety and winemakers are embracing it in many countries, so watch this space as more fine examples appear on the shelves. In California, producers who love Rhône varieties have been dubbed the 'Rhône Rangers' – sample the efforts of Bonny Doon, or Cline Cellars to judge how well they are doing. South Africa is one to watch; some of the Shiraz/Syrah coming out of the Cape at the moment is marvellously concentrated and Rhône-like, with a strong, oaky structure. Try wines from the Groot Constantia and Boekenhoutskloof wineries if you get the chance. New Zealand is a surprising source of fine Syrah – surprising because this grape needs lots of warmth and it doesn't get too hot there. But the sunny Hawke's Bay region is proving it can be successful with this variety. More plantings are set to come on stream in the next few years so look out for Kiwi Syrah. Another tip is Argentina – wines from the Mendoza region close to the Andes are causing a stir for their ripe, smooth character.

# Other full-bodied reds

**Grenache**  The Grenache grape doesn't excel at making subtle, complex, elegant reds: oh, no. This variety makes big, boisterous, joyful wines with high alcohol levels, although relatively low tannins. It tastes of sweet, plummy fruit, sometimes with a hint of chocolate and it has a dry but succulent finish. It has been used and abused in the past to make cheap-and-cheerless, disappointingly dilute wine from irrigated, high-yielding vines, but in recent years there has been a movement towards premium Grenache with loads more flavour, body and guts.

Find it in the south of France, in the Languedoc, in the Southern Rhône (as a major component of Châteauneuf-du-Pape, see above) and all along the French coast of the Med. It is often blended with Syrah and Mourvèdre. Some Australians take it seriously, particularly Charles Melton in the Barossa Valley, and the Californians are starting to show interest. But the most important country after France for this grape is Spain, where, as Garnacha, it is making increasingly serious, concentrated, powerful reds, usually from old vines. The scenic mountainous region of Priorato is the place to go for the serious monsters, although Tarragona comes a close second. Expect massive wines which may need years to open up. Masía Barril, Clos Mogador and Celliers de Capçanes are some of the wineries to look out for.

**Nebbiolo**  Nebbiolo is the grape behind Italy's huge Piedmont reds, Barolo and Barbaresco. It ripens late in the autumn, in the mist-covered hills of the region (hence the name Nebbiolo, which means 'foggy'), and it makes a dense wine with high levels of acid and tannin. There's nothing else quite like Nebbiolo, which has a savoury yet floral perfume (some spot roses) and hints of truffles, blackberry and liquorice. Many consider it to be a truly great variety. Certainly, top examples are impressive, refreshingly different and they age brilliantly. Nebbiolo is hardly ever made elsewhere, partly because mastering its high acidity and thick tannin, while prising some fruity character out, is so difficult. Aldo Conterno, Gaja, Giacosa and Roberto Voerzio are all Italian masters. Prices are high for the well-known producers and you need to beware any really poor vintages. Another hefty Italian worth a try is Amarone from Valpolicella, made from the juice of dried grapes (mostly Corvina) and gloriously thick, ripe and alcoholic. Great with cheese.

**Malbec**  Argentina's greatest success to date has been with the Malbec grape, which originally comes from Cahors but has become a minor vine in France. Immigrants planted it long ago in the Mendoza region and today it produces beautifully rich but rounded, smooth reds packed with black cherry fruit. Brilliant with steak. Quality is high from many producers.

**Tannat**  Uruguay's ace card, according to its fans. Tannat is a thick-skinned, sturdy grape, which produces leathery, highly tannic wines with mulberry fruit and toffee-rich depths. Uruguay is still fairly unknown to most wine-drinkers, but as more of its producers start exporting, look out for Tannat, which does well in the damp maritime climate of this South American country. Not all bottles containing it will please – there are too many over-chewy, tannic, thick-set examples – but it can be deliciously different. Tannat's original home is Madiran in southern France, where it again makes very tannic, near-black wine which will appeal to lovers of rich reds, but which need at least a decade in bottle before they start to open up.

**Baga and Touriga Nacional**  Two Portuguese varieties which are capable of making the most interesting and complex reds in the country. Baga is found mainly in Bairrada in northern Portugal, and is a tough grape with a thick skin which produces (you guessed it) tannic, powerful wines. In the past, many of these proved too hard and heavy-going, but modern vinification methods are turning up a new generation of Bairrada reds with softer blackberry and liquroice flavours. Try Luis Pato's wines. Touriga Nacional is found in port country, and is perhaps the most hallowed of the port grapes. Today it is the mainstay of the Dâo region and the new, often brilliant, unfortified red wines coming out of the Douro Valley, the best of which are bursting with intense flavours of red fruit and blackcurrant, with plenty of rounded but firm structure. These wines age well. Sample Quinta de la Rosa and Quinta do Crasto, among others.

**Pinotage**  South African grape developed by crossing Pinot Noir and Cinsault. There used to be a spooky amount of rough, sour, tomatoey Pinotage knocking around, but quality has improved dramatically as Cape winemakers get on top of modern methods, and many more ripe, plummy, carefully oaked wines are now appearing. Cheap Pinotage can be simple stuff, fruity and medium-bodied, but top examples are concentrated, creamily rich and very satisfying. Kanonkop is the most famous producer, but try Beyerskloof, Longridge, Simonsig and Warwick Estate, too. Great with barbecued red meats – so light the braii!

**Zinfandel**  Californian wine can get rather boring with its flood of predictably oaky, rich Chardonnays and Cabernets, so here's a welcome and refreshing change. Zinfandel ('Zin') is a West Coast speciality capable of making generously fruity, full-bodied, often highly alcoholic reds with a thick, sweetly ripe, raspberry flavour and a twist of black pepper. Most believe that it is the same grape as Italy's Primitivo and was brought over by Italian immigrants. Watch out for a few overblown, over-oaky monsters, but always avoid pink and off-white Zin in favour of red. Best producers: Ridge, Pedroncelli, Seghesio, Frog's Leap.

# shortcuts to success

## FIRST TASTE

• Many of these wines can be described as fruity, but fresh-fruit flavours certainly don't spell out the whole picture as they do in lighter styles of red. Look out for other dominant aromas and tastes. Many of the full-bodied reds are spicy – black pepper, cloves, cinnamon and nutmeg – and have whiffs of chocolate, cream and toffee, even liquorice and tar, savoury notes and herbs. Cabernet can be minty!

• Tannic reds need food – if you taste them on their own, be prepared for the structure to seem a little too firm and chewy. The same wine with a steak may seem more balanced as it will work well with the rich protein in the food.

• That said, some rich reds are out of balance, steak or no steak. Watch out for over-tannic reds which smell of freshly planed wood and taste like chewing on a tea bag. Ones with concentrated fruit and acids may soften over time, but a few are clearly just too oaky and heavy. Ditch them in favour of wines with better poise and subtlety.

• Taste these wines at room temperature, not cellar-cold and never fireside-warm.

• Open them up way before tasting to let the wine breathe – however, the more effective way to get a tough red to soften and mellow is to decant it before drinking. And swirl it around in big glasses to release its aroma.

# BUYER'S GUIDE

• Good news! There are plenty of reliable, well-priced full-bodied reds out there, including Chilean Cabernet, Australian Cabernet and Cabernet-Shiraz blends, Côtes du Rhône-Villages… Not dirt-cheap, perhaps, but with loads of food-friendly flavour and concentration for relatively little outlay.

• Very cheap hefty reds are worth avoiding. Bargain reds, even those made from Shiraz and Cabernet, almost certainly won't deliver a big personality, and may be dilute, bland or jammy.

• And tread more carefully with claret (red Bordeaux) at lower prices. It only starts to get reliable in the mid-price range and over, and you still need to pick a good year, a reputable producer, a fine wine merchant…

• The top clarets, finest Aussie Shirazes and Italian Barolos, all need time so stash them away for several years or they are a waste of money. Don't crack open expensive, rich reds unless you know they will be ready to drink. Use a specialist wine merchant and take advice on individual purchases.

# MOVING ON

• Once you've sampled enough straight, one hundred percent Cabernet and Shiraz, try the blends – most red Bordeaux, Australian Cab-Shiraz, Cabernet-Merlot from around the world – for different flavours, aromas and textures.

• Try wines from as many different parts of the Rhône Valley as you can find – this is a fascinating, multi-faceted region with a wide variety of Syrah and Grenache-based wines. Then head down to the south of France for some more big reds.

• Set up a comparative tasting of other gutsy reds – Zinfandel from California, Pinotage from South Africa, Malbec and Tannat from South America.

• See how older, full-bodied reds start to lose their tannic grip and soften with age. Some wines, like Barolo or fine claret, are fascinating to watch in development. Buy a few bottles of the same wine and open one every six months or so to track its evolution.

• Experiment with matching different dishes to big reds, as these are really food-friendly wines. Try red meat with young claret and game with older versions. Match a peppery Syrah with a hearty, slightly spicy dish, and decide which of these wines is best with mature cheese or roast lamb. Which makes the best Christmas red?

# rosés

Think pink. Rosé is a much underrated style of wine. There's nothing to compare with a frosty-cold glass of fresh, young, pink wine on a hot summer's day, yet many people simply associate rosé with sugary, old-fashioned plonk and avoid it. It's easy to see why – there are lots of badly made rosés out there.

Rosé can be made in three different ways: either the red grapes are crushed and the skins left in with the juice for several hours until the colour and flavours have leached off into the liquid, which is then fermented; or, for a lighter style, the juice is run off the skins straightaway and fermented, or, very occasionally, red wine is blended with white. Because this is a fragile type of wine not built with the structure to last well, you may come across a lot of pink that is simply past its best and tastes dull and flat. But persevere – the clever wine-buyer knows how to avoid the fading blooms, coming up rosé with the snappiest, most refreshing pinks around. Here you will find out how.

Even when you know how to spot a decent rosé, it's essential to be aware that many different styles of pink wine are made around the world. A fine, delicate rosé from the cool Loire in France is nothing like a rich, powerful Grenache rosé from South Australia. And dryness/sweetness levels vary a lot, too, so be prepared for that. Then it's essential to choose the right moment to sink some pink; perhaps more so than with any other style of wine, rosé only suits certain occasions.

Summery weather, outside dining, light salads and cold meats, fruit and mild cheeses… all these shout 'rosé!'. I never, ever want pink wine in the deep mid-winter, or with a hearty stew, or when I'm drinking by the fireside. That's probably why we all enjoy rosé on our summer holidays but rarely get a kick out of the bottle we bring home and crack open in chilly October! So, pick a pink with care, and pick the perfect moment to enjoy it.

**APPEARANCE** Rosé wine can be anything from almost white, with the very palest tinge of pink, to a bright, sunset peachy-orange, and even a deep cerise, like a light red.

**TEXTURE** The lightest rosés are thin and lean, even dilute, but the richest are weighty, almost syrupy in richness.

# rosés

**AROMA** Think of red berries – rosé should always have an appealing, fresh fragrance of raspberries, cherries, strawberries or cranberries. Some have more blackcurrant and plums on the bouquet, others smell of rosehip cordial. Look out for a subtle hint of grass on leaner styles and even a whiff of vanilla ice-cream – raspberry ripple is quite common!

**FLAVOUR** Those red berries should charge through on the palate, too, along with a creaminess on the richer styles. Some rosés have a thin, disappointingly short finish, while the chunkiest have a much more lingering flavour, like a red wine, with some slight tannin on the finish. There should always be a sense of fresh, crisp acidity in rosé. Be aware that some are bone-dry, others are medium to sweet.

# France

French rosé is still pretty popular, from the delicate pinks of the Loire Valley, to the well-balanced, fruity ones of Bordeaux, and the gutsy, rich wines of the south. Roughly speaking, the further south you head, and the warmer the vineyards become, the richer and riper the rosé gets. Across the land, though, the quality of this wine varies a lot, so choose a French rosé very carefully. Pick a good pink and you'll believe France is the master of this style, but choose a dud and you'll never bother again. Which would be a shame. Here are some hints for getting the best out of French rosé.

**LOIRE**  Let's start in the Loire Valley in north-central France, where the vineyards are cool and the pink wines more delicate, crisp and mouth-watering than those made further south. Unfortunately, this is where you are most likely to come unstuck, as the Loire, a large area with lots of subregions, churns out a wide range of rosé from delicious to dire. The pale Rosé d'Anjou is one to beware – it is often insipid and semi-sweet – instantly forgettable. Made in the area just east of the town of Ancenis, it comes from the rather uninspiring Grolleau grape, which was never destined to make great wine. Rosé d'Anjou is widely available and it is cheap, but there are many more exciting pink wines out there.

Take Cabernet d'Anjou, for example, which is made from a superior grape variety: Cabernet Franc. Like Rosé d'Anjou, it is usually off-dry, but the sweetness is matched by a riper, juicier fruitiness, and the quality overall is higher. In the Loire itself Cabernet d'Anjou is taken more seriously than other rosés. It may be harder to track down, but do try it if you get the chance. Then there's Rosé de Loire, made in Touraine and Anjou-Saumur from Cabernet Franc and sometimes other Loire grapes. This will appeal more to lovers of dry, lip-smacking, thirst-quenching styles of pink. And finally, the Vins de Pays du Jardin de la France (country wines from the Loire) provide some (usually) decent pink in the form of Cabernet Rosé, which is pleasingly light, dry and tangy, if simple.

**BORDEAUX**  Further southwest, in Bordeaux, the rosé (just like the white wine) has improved in recent years and now provides some of the most appealing pink around. The vast majority of Bordeaux rosés are made from Merlot, so you can expect some of that attractive fruity character so typical of this grape, plus (in the best wines) an attractive aroma and a crisp, succulent finish. A typical flavour is fresh strawberries with a dab of cream. A few wines have a little Cabernet Sauvignon and Cabernet Franc in the mix – here, as anywhere, rosé producers across the world make the most of any red grapes going. Bordeaux rosé is well worth trying. As usual with rosé, though, make sure to crack open a young wine. Top of any rosé-lover's list is the pink from Château de Sours.

**PROVENCE**  In the deeper south of France, Provence is the source of riper, deeply coloured rosés made mainly from Grenache and Cinsault – these wines can have a juicy rosehip and slightly toffeed character. Some arrive in traditional bottles, shaped like a bowling skittle, with a wide-hipped look to them. A fine Provence rosé is delightful and rich enough to stand up to cold meats and even Mediterranean garlic and tomato dishes, but be aware that there are lots of substandard, oxidised wines around.

**REST OF FRANCE**  Although plenty of basic table rosé is made in other parts of France, much of it is not exported but simply made to be enjoyed, young and fresh, in local bars and restaurants. Pink wines from the Charentes region are a case in point – drunk by the bucketful along the Atlantic coast to wash down *moules frites*, they are hardly ever seen outside their region. However, another couple of French pinks

## Matching rosé with food

Decent rosé is delectable on its own: truly refreshing, mouth-tingling, vibrantly fruity wine for a hot summer's day. It also partners food well, but choose carefully as very rich food will overpower its delicate flavours. A mild goat's cheese salad, a plate of cold ham (*jamón*), fresh seafood (especially prawns) and pasta with a creamy sauce all make great matches. Very cold, off-dry pink is fairly good at washing down lightly spicy dishes – vegetable samosas spring to mind.

sometimes encountered overseas are those of Tavel and Lirac in the southern Rhône Valley; these are fairly serious, chunky rosés made from the Rhône red grapes Syrah and Grenache and they taste as though they are packed with ripe red berries, perhaps with a note of spice and caramel. Good stuff. Finally, you may just come across Rosé de Riceys, a rare but delicious still pink wine made in the Champagne region from the Pinot Noir grape. It has the aroma and flavour of fresh raspberries.

# Spain

I reckon more people have been converted to rosé (or *rosado*, as it is called here) by drinking Spanish versions than any other. There's something about a chilled, tangy glass of *rosado*, enjoyed with jamón or prawns by the seaside in Spain that makes us go putty for this style of wine. As usual, we tend to bring the wine home and forget to drink it until it is old and faded, so if you enjoy Spanish *rosado in situ*, make sure you buy fresh, youthful bottles of it at home, too.

**RIOJA AND NAVARRA**  It's made in a number of regions from a range of varieties, but the best come from the Rioja and Navarra regions, usually made from either the Tempranillo or Grenache grape (called Garnacha in Spain). Expect the wine to be perfumed and cherryish, dry and mouth-watering – try Chivite's *rosado* from Navarra for a fine glassful.

**REST OF SPAIN**  Once you've tried wines from these well-known winemaking areas, go for a modern rosado from Somontano or a rich one from Priorato to ring the changes. And try the local Spanish Bobal grape which can make moreish rosado in Alicante and Utiel-Requena. Valencia's widely seen, inexpensive *rosados* are pleasantly fruity and moreish when young.

# Other European rosés

**PORTUGAL**  Portugal became famous (or should that be infamous?) for rosé with the seventies success story Mateus Rosé. The brand still exists, but nowadays the slightly off-dry, spritzy and pale pink isn't as popular as it used to be. Apart from Mateus, there are few other Portuguese rosés, although the odd one, dry and bright, from the Bairrada region makes an appearance.

**ITALY**  Italy produces a handful of palatable rosés – or *rosatos*, as they are known. As in France, the cooler areas, especially the northeast, make the crisp, pale, lighter styles, while the warmer south is responsible for richer wines. The fruity, deep-pink Cirò from Calabria, made from the local Gaglioppo grape, is one to sample.

**EASTERN EUROPE**  The occasional pink gem pops up from this region, although watch out, as standards are patchy, particularly from Bulgaria. Hungary is a better bet, making some clean, crisp and very dry cheapies.

## Storing and serving
Rosé should be consumed while it is fresh and young, as it soon loses its inviting aroma and flavour. Make sure to buy the youngest vintage you can find and never get palmed off with an elderly bottle of rosé. There's no point in cellaring rosé – drink it up soon after purchase, and once opened, keep it in the fridge and finish it within a day or two. The exceptions are the heartiest, blockbuster Aussie rosés, which may last up to a year.

# US

There's a type of pink wine made in the US which, strictly speaking, isn't. Pink, that is. It's more a pallid off-white with a faint hint of blush if you hold it up to the light. The aromas are neutral and the flavours are equally disappointing.

**CALIFORNIA** Often sweetish, and distinctly lacking in fruit flavours, these 'blush' wines are popular over there, and to a certain extent, over here, too. They are often made from the Zinfandel grape, another cause for complaint, as 'Zin' can be wonderful when made into a hearty red wine, but is decidedly disappointing when forced into producing these weak, bland semi-rosés. 'White Zinfandel', blush Zinfandel and other lookalikes are widely available on the export market, and for some people, the sweetness and blandness will be a plus, but do be aware that there are much more exciting rosé wines out there!

Even from California. You see, some of the better West Coast winemakers have now decided to make much riper, deeply coloured rosés and these wines (in my view, anyway) knock those pale blush rosés for six. Sometimes made from Syrah, occasionally from Grenache, they are pretty gutsy and rich. Try Fetzer's Syrah Rosé as a prime example of new-wave Californian pink wine.

# Australia

Anyone who hates pale and uninteresting rosé should take note – the Aussies make wonderfully rich, dark, alcoholic, no-nonsense rosé that is certainly not for wimps!

OK, so there aren't exactly hundreds of them around, but a wine like Charles Melton's Rose of Virginia, a cerise-coloured, weighty mouthful of strawberry and cranberry, with a creamy finish, proves the point. This wine is made from Grenache in the warm Barossa Valley in South Australia. Geoff Merrill, also working in South Australia, makes another strong, robust rosé, and a few slightly crisper examples are produced in cooler climes like the Yarra Valley and Tasmania. The big, buxom Aussie rosés will age for longer than most weedy pinks – a year or so in the case of Melton's wine.

# Rosés from the rest of the world

**CHILE AND ARGENTINA** These countries are not well-known for rosé, but a few tasty examples come out of both. Chile produces mainly Cabernet Sauvignon-based rosés, usually fresh and aromatic, while some wineries around the Argentinian winemaking capital of Mendoza turn out sprightly, fruity Syrah-based pinks. South American rosé can be good value for money. Try Miguel Torres' inexpensive example from Chile in the first instance.

**REST OF THE WORLD** New Zealand makes one or two worthwhile rosés, particularly in the Marlborough region of the South Island, where the wines taste light, lean and a little grassy. Merlot is usually used. Another part of the world more important for rosé, although perhaps less well-known, is North Africa. Several North African countries produce them from the Southern French grapes Grenache, Syrah and Cinsault. Morocco is the best source: the wines can be more than palatable.

shortcuts to
success

# BUYER'S GUIDE

• Although Rosé d'Anjou from the Loire Valley, France, is one of the most commonly seen rosés, it is not always the best – try other French pinks, especially Bordeaux rosé, and, if you see it, rosé from Tavel or Lirac in the Rhône Valley.

• They are usually a little more expensive than European ones, but Australian rosés are richer and heartier, and the top ones are serious bottles that would go down well at a barbie.

• Always, always, buy the youngest rosé you can find either in the shops or off a wine list. Aim for a very recent vintage. Reject anything too old or your pink will have lost its bloom.

# FIRST TASTE

• Be aware that rosé is a fragile wine and loses its fruity flavours sooner than most. Always buy and drink it up soon after bottling – and once opened, don't leave rosé hanging around. Either finish it within twenty-four hours or ditch it!

• Pick your moment to crack a bottle open as rosé suits hot-weather drinking, either with no food at all, or with light snacks and salads. This is not a wine to drink with rich, hearty dishes.

• Always serve rosé well-chilled – even colder than you might serve rich white wines as the chill emphasises the refreshing, tangy nature of the wine. Frosty glasses of icy rosé always look appealing.

# MOVING ON

• For party pinks, try Chilean or Argentinian rosés. There aren't too many around, but they are good value and make a change from French or Spanish ones.

• Move on from boring basic Californian 'blush' and trade up to the new-wave, gutsy West Coast rosés with bags more colour and flavour.

• Try Moroccan rosé, which is surprisingly tasty from a country not exactly renowned for its winemaking prowess!

# sparkling wines

Sparkling wine puts more consumers in a dither than any other style. What is Champagne, exactly? Should I always buy Champagne, or will a cheap fizz do just as well? Do I have to spend a fortune on a famous label? How do I open the bottle, let alone store and serve it? Does it go with food? Wine with bubbles costs a lot more than wine without (I'll explain why later on), so it is understandable that we want to know exactly how best to spend our precious pennies.

The pressure to get it right, of course, is only exacerbated by the fact that fizz is usually brought out on special occasions. Ironically, this means we often fail to notice its shortcomings. People might sweat over which bubbly to serve at their darling daughter's wedding, but on the big day itself, everyone is far too busy chattering, listening to speeches and dancing to notice a painfully thin and acidic wine in their glass – unpleasant traits they may have spotted had they cracked open a bottle one quiet Tuesday night. Still, think hard, I'm sure you will remember a moment when an expensive fizz has disappointed. There are plenty of hints on the following pages to help you avoid a repeat performance and instead make Champagne and sparkling wines enhance life's most joyful moments.

Certainly, there is nothing else in the wine world to touch Champagne for glamour and kudos. The packaging is often ornate and classy, the brands glittering and famous, the price tag scarily high. It all adds to the impression that you are buying a touch of luxury. But I wish we took sparkling wine less seriously in the UK. Go to Australia and they crack open a bottle of inexpensive, locally produced bubbly on an everyday basis, yet still drink Champagne on a momentous occasion. We should do the same. Fizzy wine comes in so many different styles and at so many different price points that we deserve to ring the changes more often. Let your life sparkle a little more!

**APPEARANCE** Most sparklers are pale and straw-coloured, although pink fizz ranges from a delicate onion-skin hue to a rich, sunset crimson. Red sparklers are a rich garnet. The look of the bubbles is important, too: they should be tiny, rather than large and coarse, and there should be plenty of them.

**TEXTURE** Champagne can be pretty rich and complex, but the high acidity and fine streams of tiny bubbles give a light impression and a refreshing lift to the wine.

# sparkling wines

**AROMA** There's a fresh, fruity perfume, often lemons, sometimes more orangey or appley, with hints of peaches and raspberries (especially in rosé). A lot of fizz has a distinct yeastiness, too, which sometimes comes across as fresh bread, brioche or even Marmite. Look out for creamy, yoghurty aromas, as well as biscuit in some sparklers and milk chocolate in others.

**FLAVOUR** Crisp, tangy acidity is a must in a good sparkler to give a refreshing, mouth-watering finish. As with the aromas, that fresh, clean fruit is there, as are the same hints of yeast, yoghurt and chocolate, particularly on the finish. Champagne is sometimes described as having a 'double' taste: a clean, incisively crisp attack followed by richer, creamier depths after swallowing.

# France

First things first. Champagne is only Champagne when it comes from the Champagne region of northeast France. Any other bubbly is sparkling wine and so must not use the 'Ch...' word on its label.

CHAMPAGNE At the top end of the quality ladder, the best Champagne is still the most gorgeous sparkler in the world. Why is it so special? Firstly, the Champenois have been making sparkling wine for centuries – ever since monks there discovered how to create bubbles, probably by mistake, in the seventeenth century – so they have a high level of expertise. Rules and regulations exist to ensure a certain level of quality (though there have been good and bad times for general Champagne quality). Most important are the natural conditions in this part of France – the chalky soils, the cool climate – that help to create a thin, acidic base wine. When put through a second fermentation with the resulting bubbles trapped in the liquid and aged in the bottle, this creates sparkling wine of finesse and complexity.

The best Champagnes combine a certain amount of power – plenty of rich fruit, layers of rich cream, yeast, bread and chocolate – with remarkable elegance: a fine and enchanting balance. They are among the most effective appetite-whetters in the world, with mouth-watering crispness and palate-teasing bubbles, and yet they go well with seafood, fish and even light chicken and vegetarian dishes. Some Champagnes are at their most delightful when young and vivacious, while others age and mellow gracefully into more honeyed, toffeed wines with a mere prickle of gas on the tongue. No wonder Champagne is still so revered and adored around the world. Most other sparklers seem unsubtle and clumsy by comparison.

That said – and you probably knew this was coming – there are still plenty of poor Champagnes that let the side down, though fewer than there used to be. The main problems are sour acidity, high enough to create an involuntary wince, and what has been described as a 'lean, mean, green' character. In other words, a lack of ripeness and a reliance on very young wine in the blend, rather than extra-aged reserve blending wine. In the late eighties and early nineties, these cheap and nasty Champagnes seemed to proliferate. After protests from critics and consumers, the Champenois successfully raised their general quality.

To avoid the tooth-rotting nasties that still lurk out there, give the very cheapest Champagnes a miss (switch to other types of sparkling wine at reasonable prices), but pick a reliable name and never drink vintage Champagne when it is too young. Although non-vintage – a blend from different years – is meant to be consumed soon after release, vintage should be kept for several years after purchase or it can taste raw and tart. For example, the superb 1990s are drinking well at the time of writing: thirteen years after the grapes were harvested.

The meticulous, time-consuming technique for producing Champagne is called the *méthode traditionnelle*, also known as *méthode champenoise*, and used throughout the region. The basic wine is put into heavy bottles, which must be thick or they would crack under the pressure of the gassy wine, then a little yeast and sugar solution is introduced and the bottle sealed with a metal cap. The wine re-ferments, trapping the carbon dioxide produced in the liquid, and the sediment of dead yeast, also known as the lees, settles. The wine is left to age on its lees, which gives it some yeasty character and richness. The bottles are turned regularly on a rack and twisted at an ever-sharper angle, gradually moving to an upside-down position, with the sediment resting in the neck of the bottle. At the end of this process, the neck is frozen and the bottle opened to release the solid plug

## Making the difference

The *méthode traditionnelle*, or Champagne method, is described above. Other less laborious and cheaper ways to produce fizz include the transfer method, with second fermentation in the bottle, followed by disgorgement into large tanks to remove the sediment, then the addition of sugar solution and rebottling. There is also the tank method, with second fermentation in large pressure tanks to which sugar and yeast have been added, and perhaps even the crudest method of all, pumping carbon dioxide into the liquid to create bubbles. These methods don't produce such good quality fizz and in the case of the last method, makes fairly unpleasant stuff!

of frozen sediment. It is then topped up with a little *dosage*, or sweetened wine, the amount and contents of which help determine the style of the finished wine. Finally the bottle is re-sealed, but this time with the distinctive Champagne cork and wire cage. *Et voilà!*

This careful, slow process has been adopted for fine sparkling wines all over the world. Likewise, the same classic Champagne blend of grapes is sometimes used: Chardonnay, Pinot Noir and Pinot Meunier are the only three grapes allowed in Champagne. The first two are the most important and appear either together in a blend or occasionally as single-varietal wines. A bottle labelled *blanc de blancs* Champagne is made from one hundred percent Chardonnay whereas one labelled

*blanc de noirs* (literally, white from blacks) is one hundred percent Pinot grapes (Noir and Meunier, usually). *Blanc de blancs* tends to be creamier with yellow-fruit flavours, *blanc de noirs* has a red-berry, particularly raspberry, character and is firmer and more aromatic. No one style is necessarily better than another, so go for the wine you like best.

The famous Champagne houses do not necessarily offer the best value for money, considering the prohibitively high prices many of them fetch. Supermarket own-label Champagnes are very reasonable and have improved enormously over the past decade; in fact, many of them are now sourced from highly reputable Champagne producers. But

## Matching sparkling wines with food

Most of us can't wait to crack open a bottle of fizz and drink it on its own as a toast, a celebration or a seduction tool. But hold on a second. Although *brut*, with its crisp acidity and refreshing bubbles, is a great aperitif, it is also a good partner for light canapés, seafood, fish dishes and, in the case of the richest wines, even light chicken recipes. Try sweeter styles of sparkling wine with fresh fruit and light desserts. Dry rosé makes a good partner for seafood, especially prawns.

sometimes we all prefer to shell out more money for a glamorous label. Among the best of the swanky labels to go for – the ones consistently providing the most delectable wines as well as stylish packaging – are Moët et Chandon, Veuve Clicquot, Bollinger, Louis Roederer, Krug, Billecart-Salmon, Charles Heidsieck, Lanson, Pol Roger, Ruinart and Taittinger. Less well-known but impressive Champagne houses include Joseph Perrier, Jacquesson, the cooperative Jacquart and Gosset. Also, look out for wines made by the grape-growers themselves as these often offer terrific value for money. Good 'grower' Champagnes include Gimonnet and Goutorbe.

The vast majority of bottles sold are *brut* (dry), but do give other styles of Champagne a whirl. To enjoy them at their best, try each at the right moment. *Demi-sec* (sweeter with honeyed overtones) is lovely served with fruit puddings or cakes – it's certainly better with wedding cake than *brut*. *Sec* is in between the previous two styles, so serve it with somewhat sweet-tasting savoury canapés, perhaps pâté or seafood. Rosé is a delight, usually made by adding small amounts of red Pinot Noir wine from the Bouzy or Aÿ areas of Champagne to the blend. It is fruitier, tasting overtly of red berries and peaches, and goes well with prawns, salmon and lobster. And of course, it is the ultimate in romantic drinks.

Serve all Champagnes well-chilled and drink up soon after opening; otherwise they will go a little flat quickly. There are various methods for keeping Champagne fizzy overnight, but in my view, nothing quite tastes the same as a freshly opened, fabulously fizzy bottle.

**CRÉMANT** For Francophiles who don't want to splash out on Champagne, or if you want a cheaper fizz for everyday drinking, *crémant* is the next best thing. This category of French fizz was created in the 1980s with the aim of providing regulated, good-quality bubbly made in the *méthode traditionnelle*, but from other parts of France.

As with Champagne, there are certain rules and regulations that apply to *crémant* production and, although different grape varieties are permitted in different areas, in very general terms, the results are pretty impressive considering the relatively low prices charged. Crémant d'Alsace is clean, tangy and fresh, rather leaner and more mineral in style than Champagne. Crémant de Bourgogne tends to be made from Chardonnay and Pinot Noir – the same grapes as Champagne – and is aromatic with fruity, red-berry flavours. Crémant de Loire is lemony, zingy and has a crisp mousse. Crémant de Limoux is refreshing, creamy… And so on. Many people discover a local *crémant* while on holiday in France, so if you stumble across one at home or abroad, then do give it a go.

**REST OF FRANCE** Sadly, there is an ocean of cheap and very nasty fizz made in France. That bargain bottle with a plastic stopper, bought in Calais with some spare change, may well turn out to be sickly sweet and artificial tasting or, even worse, metallic or rubbery in character. Buyer beware! My strong advice to those stocking up for a special occasion is always, but always, try one bottle of cheap fizz before committing to a boot-load. And do sample a wine called Clairette de Die Tradition or Clairette de Die Méthode Dioise Ancestrale, if you see them. Produced around the town of Die on the River Drôme, a tributary of the Rhône, these are gently frothy, grapily refreshing, off-dry sparklers made partly with the perfumed Muscat grape. They are great with cakes and fruit.

# Spain

One of the most common misconceptions surrounding fizz is that cava is a type of sparkling wine made around the world. It is, in fact, a purely Spanish wine. Like sherry and Rioja, cava is one of this country's great classics.

**CAVA** Cava is typically fresh, dry and fairly neutral, with appley notes and sometimes a mineral quality. It may not be especially exciting, but as such it is refreshing, reliable and remarkably well-priced.

Cava is produced mainly in the region of Penedés, on the eastern edge of Spain, and is made in the same laborious way as Champagne, which is quite astonishing when you consider the price difference between wines from the two regions. Cava is not made from the same grapes as Champagne, though. Instead, a trio of local Spanish grapes is used – Macabeo, Parellada and Xarel-lo – although some quality-conscious (and fashion-conscious) producers include Chardonnay in the blend to add a modern, rounded and fruity note. Wines are made and aged in the huge cellars that lie under the town of San Sadurni de Noya.

Vintage cava from one fine year is a treat for sparkling-wine lovers. The best examples, from a top producer like Juvé y Camps, taste richer and more rounded but with that same sprightly apple character at the core, and not a bit like Champagne. The enormous popularity of cava is still growing, despite the threat from non-European bubblies. Cava now accounts for nearly fifty percent of the sparkling-wine market in the UK. That's an awful lot of bubbles. As long as prices stay low, and the cheapest supermarket own-label bottles remain so reliable, we shall continue to adore this wine.

# Italy

I always feel confident when I see Italian Prosecco offered as the house fizz on a restaurant wine list. I can be pretty sure of getting a dry, mouthwatering aperitif with plenty of crisp bubbles, a slightly floral, violetty aroma and fresh, sherbetty flavours. What's more, I will pay around half the price of a glass of Champagne.

**PROSECCO** Prosecco is Italy's most moreish fizz, made from the grape variety of the same name around the hills of Treviso in Veneto, to the northeast. The best wines are labelled 'Superiore di Cartizze'. Look for the word *frizzante* on the label as this means a style with a gentler mousse – more froth than fizz.

**ASTI** Asti is perhaps a more famous Italian sparkling wine. Snobs are often patronising about this sweet, grapey wine – not officially called Spumante anymore, but now simply Asti – but its many fans find it sadly underrated. Certainly, a fresh, youthful Asti served frostily cold with desserts, cakes, sweet biscuits or on its own at the end of a rich feast is wonderfully uplifting and palate-cleansing. Its naturally low alcohol is a bonus, too, after lots of other, more heady wines. All too often, however, it is served at room temperature as an aperitif when a dry fizz would be so much more appealing. Save Asti's reputation, and drink it at the right moment.

If you still think it sounds naff, try its superior cousin Moscato d'Asti, which is a little less sweet with a softer, spritzier mousse. It is slightly higher in alcohol and costs a little more, but is generally more delicious and is taken a bit more seriously by wine buffs.

## Storing and serving

As a rule of thumb, cheap fizz needs drinking up quickly or it will lose its fresh appeal. Open non-vintage cava, most non-European sparklers and most non-vintage Champagne within a few weeks of purchase. The poshest non-vintage Champagne will last longer, say, up to eighteen months, as will the finest vintage cava and superior non-European sparkling wine. Top vintage Champagne, as well as one or two of California's finest, is meant to be cellared, or stashed in any cool, dark place, for several years. It will emerge a more well-knit, mellow wine with less harsh acidity and a slightly richer, more honeyed quality. Well worth the wait, in other words.

# Other European sparklers

**GERMANY AND AUSTRIA**  Germany and Austria both make sparkling wines labelled Sekt, usually from Riesling, Pinot Blanc and Welschriesling varieties. Watch out for cheap and nasty German examples that are often sulphurous; think burnt rubber or struck matches – very unpleasant. Occasionally a tasty example comes our way, and any visitor to Vienna may well enjoy a glass of cold Sekt in a bar. There's something about Sekt that makes it nicer *in situ* than at home, and anyway, its fragile nature means it doesn't travel well. The best you can expect, however, is a zesty, dry, bubbly mouthful. The Austrian producer Bründlmayer makes the finest Sekt I have come across.

**ENGLAND**  Recently, England has become the unlikely source of some rather exciting sparkling wines made in the traditional method (see the 'Champagne' section on page 134–5). Or is it so unlikely? England's cool climate, which not so very different from that of the Champagne region in northern France, and the chalky soils in parts of the south make it ideal for producing a simple, tart, base wine for fizz. English winemakers are rapidly developing their skills for sparklers and the result is bumper crop of quality bubblies, some of which have won awards in international competitions for their poise and elegance. Let's hear it for Nyetimber, Ridgeview and Valley Vineyards, among others, championing English sparklers effectively for the first time.

# Sparklers from the rest of the world

There are now some super sparklers from the newer parts of the winemaking globe: New Zealand, Australia, California and so on. There are three interesting facts to note here, however. One, the *méthode traditionnelle* is widely employed to create the best examples, as are the two most important grape varieties used in Champagne – Chardonnay and Pinot Noir.

Secondly, Champagne houses are heavily involved in the production of much of the finest overseas fizz. Louis Roederer's offshoot in California, which makes a wine called Quartet; Deutz Marlborough Cuvée in New Zealand; and Moët et Chandon's Green Point from Australia, are all cases in point. Even Cloudy Bay's classy, rich sparkler, Pelorus, has some input from Veuve Clicquot. Clearly the Champenois know a good opportunity when they see one and believe there is a healthy market out there for both Champagne and sparkling wine.

Thirdly, southern-hemisphere winemakers have only become successful at fizz since they started sourcing grapes from cool-climate vineyards. Hot spots simply don't make fizz with finesse.

**AUSTRALIA**  Take Australian bubbly, for example. There are lots of ripe, sunny, big-bubbled Aussie sparklers, made mainly by cheaper modes of production than the Champagne method. For refined, well-balanced sparkling wine from this country you need grapes – Chardonnay and Pinot Noir, naturally – grown in cool areas such as Tasmania, the Yarra Valley in Victoria and the Adelaide Hills in South Australia. Some wines made from such fruit are really starting to show class: try Pirie from the Tasmanian winery Piper's Brook, Domaine Chandon's Green Point and Yalumba 'D' for some impressive wine.

Some of the cheap-and-cheerful bubblies made by the less expensive methods are actually fine for everyday glugging; Yalumba's Angas Brut has always been reliably fun and fruity. Also, don't miss the chance to try Sparkling Shiraz, purple froth with soft, curranty fruit. Served cold with a barbecue or even on Christmas Day, it can be a jolly and unusual way to drink bubbly. (Just avoid popping the cork over new pale carpets, though…)

**NEW ZEALAND** New Zealand is an exciting place for fizz. The Marlborough region on the South Island has the right conditions – a long, cool ripening season – suitable for Chardonnay and Pinot base wine. It provides some good-value labels with pure, bright fruit flavours and crisp acidity – in fact, typical of the region's still wines. Hunter's Miru Miru, Huia's Brut, Cloudy Bay Pelorus and Deutz Marlborough Cuvée are some of the most interesting.

**SOUTH AFRICA** South Africa makes sparklers by the traditional Champagne methoda, which it calls Méthode Cap Classique, or MCC. Despite the fact that some of the packaging is old-fashioned and garish, Cape sparklers can be surprisingly good, even from warmer spots. Graham Beck leads the way with his range from the hot spot of Robertson, and winemakers from the pretty valley of Franschhoek have come up with impressively fresh and snappy wines in the past. Some inexpensive,

non-MCC Cape fizz has been successful in export markets. These are made mainly by the cheaper methods of production and from grapes other than Chardonnay and Pinot Noir. Brands such as Kumala and Arniston Bay may be popular, but they lack finesse and character. Stick to MCC wines if you can trade up a notch or two.

**US** California is home to some highly successful producers of refined sparkling wine, made by the Champagne method and from the Champagne grapes. The cooler spots, such as Carneros and Anderson Valley, turn out superb grapes for fizz. Some of these wines are very classy indeed. Try the Champagne offshoot wineries Roederer Estate (Quartet) and Cuvée Napa Mumm. Other labels to look out for include Jordan's 'J' and Schramsberg. Watch out for the prices, though; their quality may occasionally rival that of Champagne, but then so can their price tags.

There aren't many decent sparklers made in South America that I can recommend. You may just pick up a decent fizz from Canada, New York State's Finger Lakes or Oregon, but you are more likely to come across these wines when you are visiting the area, rather than in your local supermarket.

## shortcuts to success

## FIRST TASTE

• Look out for different levels of richness. Some sparklers are distinctly lean and green with unappetisingly high acidity. Better bottles have a riper, creamier quality, more layers of flavour and a lingering finish. Avoid the high-acid monsters!

• Try sweeter styles of sparkling wine – *demi-sec* or even the slightly less dry *sec*. *Brut* accounts for most of the fizz sold, but there are some occasions when sweeter sparklers are more appropriate. Fizz comes in unusual styles, too – not just *brut*, white and French. Try an English sparkler, a sweet, frothy Moscato d'Asti, or a red sparkling Shiraz from Australia.

• If you ever get the chance, sample mature vintage Champagne. Most is consumed too young, so tasting one that is ten years or more in age can be revelation – a quite different experience to endless bottles of youthful fizz. Look out for rich, honeyed, even toasty nuances.

• Avoid ultra-cheap French fizz, as it is often horrible. For better quality, go for Champagne or French *crémant*.

• Always, always serve sparkling wine and Champagne chilled and soon after opening the bottle. Old, warm fizz is plain horrible!

## BUYER'S GUIDE

• Avoid very cheap, discounted Champagne from an unknown label. It may well be thin and over-acidic. Instead, go for a non-European sparkling wine or cava for inexpensive everyday bubbles.

• Some well-known supermarket own-label Champagnes are, however, good value for money. Don't anticipate great complexity, but you should be able to get a satisfying crisp, elegant sparkler for your money. Try one bottle before committing to a wedding-load, though.

• Cava is one of the best party wines there is. It is almost always fresh, dry, crisp and neutral – perfect for fuelling a big bash. Serve on its own, mixed with orange juice for Buck's Fizz or with crème de cassis for pretend Kir Royales.

• Crémant is a good-value alternative to Champagne. Quality varies a bit, but you should find something palatable for a good price.

• New Zealand also offers excellent sparklers, which are fruity and lively in style, probably the best of all in the mid-price bracket.

• California sparkling wine can be fabulous stuff, but it will cost a lot. Still, splash out on a top West Coast wine for a special occasion as a suitable alternative to fine Champagne.

## MOVING ON

• Once you are familiar with the distinctive characteristics of Champagne, try wines from different houses, not just the well-known ones. Sample some less famous names and the growers and producers who grow their own grapes. Some are mentioned in this chapter.

• Age some decent vintage Champagne. Some people like very mature Champagne, others prefer it more youthful and sprightly. Find out which suits you best. If you can afford it, stash away a few bottles and open one each New Year to see when it reaches the optimum stage of development for you.

• Don't just drink it on its own, try matching Champagne with food. Simple light canapés, fish and chicken are all easy matches. Try caviar, sushi and mildly spicy Asian dishes with fizz, too.

• Test out the best names from Australia, California and even England, places where they are now capable of making serious sparkling wine. Does it match up to Champagne, in your view?

# sweet wines

Aahh, sweet wines. Gorgeous, luscious, seductive, sticky sweet wines. The perfect partners for puddings… or even instead of pudding. On the other hand, there are sickly sweet wines, tooth-rotting glasses of dull gloop, like sugar-water, that spoil dessert and are undrinkable on their own – the sort of bottles that get passed from one charity raffle to the next. No one can think of an occasion on which to drink it, and no one would be seen dead with such an old-fashioned drink in their wine rack.

So, will the real sweet wines please stand up? Ambrosial or awful? This is certainly a style with an image problem. Sweet wines have not been in vogue for quite some time. Sure enough, there are some truly terrible examples around. Making your way round the world of dessert wines – aka pudding wines, sweet wines, stickies or sweeties – is something of a minefield. There are some weird and wonderful sweet wines out there. Certainly the way in which some of these wines are made is weird, as we shall see, but when you get a good one – a well-made Sauternes, perhaps, or fine Austrian Beerenauslese – you can see what all the fuss is about. There's something about the pairing of a wonderful dessert, let's say, a sumptuous homemade chocolate mousse, with a small, frosted glass of perfectly chilled sweet wine that is quite sublime. And rather impressive, it must be said, at the end of a grand dinner party.

Lots of keen wine fans seem to find this particular style rather complicated and daunting. However, knowing just a little about the types of wines that fall into this category will help enormously; you can avoid the nasties and sup on nectar providing you follow a few simple guidelines. Then there's value for money. Some sweet wines are incredibly off-puttingly expensive. The good news is it doesn't have to be so. There are fairly cheap bottles out there that are absolutely fine, so it pays to know which ones will do when mature Sauternes from a top château is simply not an option. Now, let's get on with the tips for an altogether sweeter experience.

**TEXTURE** Much richer and
thicker than dry white wines. Expect
a honeyed texture, almost viscous.
In some very rich and particularly
mature pudding wines, the texture
can be quite treacley.

**APPEARANCE** The
majority of dessert wines, including
those from Bordeaux, the Loire,
German and Austrian Rieslings, are
a deep, bright-gold colour – some
more deep in colour than others.
A few pudding wines are ruddy red
or mahogany brown.

# sweet wines

AROMA Some have pronounced floral scents: for example, jasmine is typical of Muscat. The aroma is fruity, too; apricot and peach, lemon and orange are common. You may notice a toffee note, or sometimes a nutty one.

FLAVOUR More apricot, plenty of honey, beeswax, barley sugar, preserved lemons and quinces, with a crisp, clean finish. That's in the good ones, anyway. Poor examples are simple concoctions of sugar and acid.

# France

Although it is more famous for its reds, the region of Bordeaux on the southwest coast of France can lay claim to some of the best sweet wines in the world. And with some justification. The appellation of Sauternes, its vineyards clustered around the River Ciron, produces wonderfully complex, finely balanced wines. They are lusciously sweet, yet have a clean, succulent acidity with something extra – the extraordinary set of characteristics that appears when a sweet wine is made from grapes with noble rot.

**SAUTERNES** Noble rot? To develop an appreciation of fine dessert wines, it is essential to understand noble rot and the part it plays in creating them, not only in Sauternes but also in certain other parts of the world. Admittedly it sounds like a contradiction: how can a rotten grape be the slightest bit 'noble'? How can such a grape produce these majestic sweet wines? Well, here's how: in certain natural conditions, the mould *Botrytis cinerea* attacks ripe grapes as they hang on the vines in the autumn. Unlike any other mould, botrytis relieves the grape of its water content, thereby concentrating the sugar, preserving the acidity and adding some strange but nonetheless delicious characteristics of its own – a slightly decayed, rich, waxy texture and flavour, like apricots drizzled with honeycomb along with a hint of a rotting autumnal forest floor... except much nicer!

The grapes are picked – sometimes one by one, a painstaking and expensive task – and fermentation starts. High sugar levels mean this is a slow process, because it takes the yeast a long time to get through all that sweetness. Eventually the yeast dies and the wine is left with loads of residual sweetness, as well as a fresh acidity to balance it out. So there you have botrytised wine, which most buffs consider the finest form of sweet wine. Sauternes is one of the few places where this rot strikes with regularity (see 'Making the difference' opposite for more on this) and it is certainly the most hallowed region on the globe for botrytised wines.

There are five villages in the region that can use the name 'Sauternes' on a label: Sauternes itself, Barsac, Bommes, Fargues and Preignac. Barsac is also entitled to its own appellation, which has a loyal following, too. Great producers of both include Yquem, de Fargues, Doisy-Daëne, Coutet and Climens. There are some cheaper alternatives in the Bordeaux area: Loupiac and Ste-Croix-du-Mont, for example, or Monbazillac and Saussignac, both near Bergerac, which provide particularly good-value sweet wines. Wines labelled 'Graves Supérieures' or 'Premières Côtes de Bordeaux' provide more rich pickings.

**LOIRE** Further north, France's Loire Valley is another famous dessert wine region. Here Chenin Blanc is used, providing wines with a honeyed, apple and quince character as well as a very distinctive clean note of acid. Because of their high sugar and acidity, some of these wines age for decades – centuries, some would say – and so, if you're planning to start a cellar, Loire sweet wines should certainly be on your shopping list.

For those who enjoy just a touch of sweetness, rather than those unctuous wines that ooze sugar, go for the *demi-sec* (medium-dry) or *doux* wines (medium-sweet) from the Loire, and Vouvray in particular. It should be noted, however, that it is sometimes, but not always, difficult to tell exactly how dry or sweet a Loire wine is from the label. The most exciting and sought-after Loire sweet wines are the botrytis-affected Chenins of appellations such as

Bonnezeaux, Quarts de Chaume and the Coteaux de Layon. Try Domaine des Baumard, Château de Fesles or Huët for a taste of the best.

ALSACE France provides a fascinating range of sweet wines, so don't stop sampling here. Alsace makes two styles: the ripe, rich, late-harvest wine *vendange tardive* and the botrytis-affected *sélection des grains nobles* wines. Beware of two pitfalls: vendange tardive bottles are sometimes medium-sweet, other times drier, and *sélection des grains nobles* wines are not widely available, partly because botrytis rot does not occur with great regularity in Alsace. If you get the chance to try the latter, jump at it. These wines – especially those made from the opulent, spicy Gewurztraminer grape – are often brilliant. Try bottles from Hugel or Zind-Humbrecht.

REST OF FRANCE Then there are French Muscats. Sweet fortified wines (see also the section 'Fortified Wines' on pages 156–167), made from the genuinely 'grapey' Muscat variety, are produced in the south of France and appear as Muscat de Beaumes-de-Venise, Muscat de St-Jean de Minervois and Muscat de Rivesaltes. These can be excellent value for money. They may lack the complexity and ageing potential of the great botrytis French dessert wines, but they are generally fresh and well-balanced, with a slightly toffeed note and act well as more 'everyday' dessert wines.

Serious sweet wine fans should also know that there are sweet fortified red wines made from the Grenache grape produced in the south, too: in Banyuls, Maury and Rivesaltes to be precise. Although they don't do it for me, I know plenty of discerning drinkers who love these wines, usually serving them with chocolate. Jurançon is our final stop in France, an area in the deep southwest that produces largely undiscovered but delicious, relatively light, fragrant sweet wines, not affected by botrytis.

## Making the difference

Botrytis rot (see opposite) can be frustrating for winemakers hoping it will strike. It appears only in certain parts of the world, and then with alarming infrequency. Note how the parts of the globe that make the best dessert wines are near bodies of water – Bordeaux, the Rhine, Neusiedler See in Austria, the Loire. Proximity to water and the humidity that brings mean it is more likely that botrytis will form.

# Germany

Forget Germany's cheap, insipid, off-dry whites in favour of her exquisitely wrought botrytised dessert wines made from the Riesling grape.

There's a fragility to these wines – low alcohol levels and an elegant apple or citrus note – that is in contrast to the striking acidity. The end result is a wonderfully refreshing wine with a mineral, almost nervily fresh and racy streak. Some people describe a 'sweet-and-sour' note, others point to a toffee-apple quality. These wines age well, turning honeyed and even a little petrolly in aroma. Cellar them away for a few years if possible.

Look out for the words *Auslese*, *Beerenauslese* or *Trockenbeerenauslese* on the label; these terms indicate quality wines of various grades of ripeness and sweetness. *Auslese* means a somewhat more delicate style, which is a little less sugary,

*Beerenauslese* is sweeter and *Trockenbeerenauslese*, or TBA, is even more luscious and ambrosial. The latter can be similar in flavour and aroma to marmalade. The best come from the Mosel region. Top names include Mönchhof, Heymann-Löwenstein, Dr. Loosen, Max Ferd Richter and J.J. Prüm.

Finally, don't miss *Eiswein*, a speciality made from the juice of frozen grapes. These are picked before dawn – presumably by masochistic winemakers – when the grapes are hard with ice. The result is scarce amounts of pure, clean-tasting sweet wine, almost an elixir, with intense sweetness and clarity. It's ridiculously rare and expensive.

# Other European sweet wines

**AUSTRIA** The Austrians make sophisticated dessert wines to rival the best from France and Germany. The best are the botrytis-affected sweeties made from a range of grape varieties around the shores of the Neusiedler See, a huge, shallow lake in Burgenland. Riesling and Grüner Veltliner appear to make the finest dessert wines in Austria. As in Germany, the grades *Beerenauslese*, *Trockenbeerenauslese* and *Eiswein* are used, but there is another category, *Ausbruch*, which lies in between the last two. *Ausbruch* is speciality of the town of Rust on the Neusiedler See and is traditionally made by adding fresh grapes to fermented must to reactivate fermentation. *Schilfwein* is another local speciality, made from grapes that have been dried on reed mats before crushing. Austrian dessert wines are, loosely speaking, high quality, good value and well worth a punt. They have a lovely, clean, fruit-compôte character

and age well. Alcohol levels are higher than in Germany while acidity is a little lower. Try wines from Kracher, Feiler-Artinger, Helmut Lang and Willi Opitz.

**HUNGARY** The dry whites and reds of Hungary may be fairly basic, but one gem really shines out from this country. Tokaji, or Tokay, is a legendary sweet wine said to have revived kings on their death beds. It is a rich, golden-amber colour and has nuances of nuts, apricot jam, marmalade and caramel. It has been made in northeastern Hungary, around the town of Mád, for centuries and has recently undergone a happy revival, with much overseas investment in ancient companies. Tokaji is made from the Furmint and Hárslevelú grapes, with a little Yellow Muscat, following a unique process. A paste made from botrytis affected grapes is added by the basket-load to a fermented base wine. A basket of paste is called a *puttonyos*, and the higher the number

## Matching sweet wines with food

Successful wine and food matching is all about balancing similar characteristics in both elements. Here, of course, the trick is to consider exactly how sweet your dessert is and find a pudding wine to match. A fresh fruit dessert with plenty of acid needs a light, crisp, not-hugely-honeyed wine, while a gloopy cream and chocolate concoction needs a very sticky, rich, treacly wine. Try botrytis wines, especially Sauternes and Alsace dessert wines, with luxurious, smooth pâtés and even with salty blue cheese. Roquefort and Sauternes is a classic and heavenly marriage.

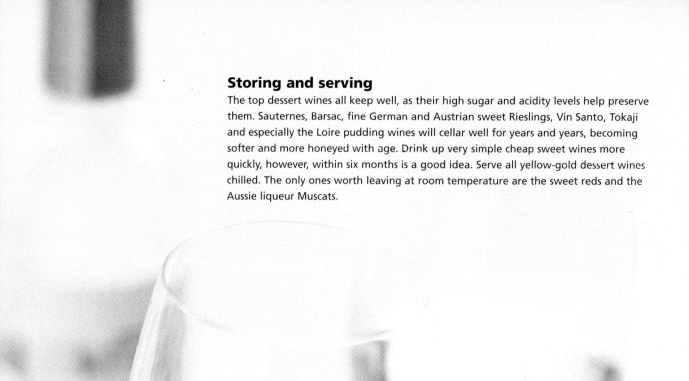

## Storing and serving

The top dessert wines all keep well, as their high sugar and acidity levels help preserve them. Sauternes, Barsac, fine German and Austrian sweet Rieslings, Vin Santo, Tokaji and especially the Loire pudding wines will cellar well for years and years, becoming softer and more honeyed with age. Drink up very simple cheap sweet wines more quickly, however, within six months is a good idea. Serve all yellow-gold dessert wines chilled. The only ones worth leaving at room temperature are the sweet reds and the Aussie liqueur Muscats.

of *puttonyos* added, the sweeter and stickier the wine. Always go for a bottled labelled five *puttonyos* or more, and perhaps even attempt the fabled Tokaji Eszencia (eight *puttonyos*) at some point. Tokaji is a superb partner for chocolate. Domaine Disznókö, Château Megyer and The Royal Tokay Wine Company are some of the producers to go for.

**ITALY**  Italy's *vin santo*, or holy wine, is produced mainly in Tuscany in the *passito* style: in other words, from shrivelled grapes that have been left to dry after picking and are then squeezed of their concentrated, raisiny syrup. Expect a rich intensity of citrus fruit, peaches and nut oil. Other intriguing Italian sweeties include Marsala (see also the section on 'Fortified Wines' on pages 156–167), the *recioto* wines of Valpolicella (reds made from dried grapes to give a port-like wine), the Recioto di Soave (the same principle applied to white grapes) and the ambrosial Passito di Pantelleria (made from Muscat grapes, here called Zibbibo, on the island of Pantelleria). Oh, and don't forget sweet, frothy Asti and Moscato d'Asti (dealt with more fully in the 'Sparkling Wines' section on page 138).

**SPAIN**  Spain deserves a mention for the Moscatels of Valencia: sweet wines made from the Muscat grape inland from the east coast. These are consistently fresh, appealing, but rather simple wines. They are a good idea if you are on a tight budget and are likewise recommended in recipes that call for decent sweet wine, such as poached pears.

**ENGLAND**  England is producing one or two impressive sweeter whites today. Watch out for more as English winemaking grows more confident.

# Sweet wines from the rest of the world

Plenty of ripe, fruity sweet wines come from the newer winemaking countries. An EU directive that prevented these wines being imported into Europe – presumably to protect our own producers – has been gradually loosened so it is now a great deal easier to source these wines at home, although often from specialist merchants.

**CANADA**  Canada is one of the finest sweet wine producers in the world. Made from frozen grapes in a similar way to European *Eiswein*, its Icewine is a rare but delectable nectar with intricate layers of fruit flavour, sweetness and acidity.

**AUSTRALIA**  Australia puts some botrytised Semillons and Rieslings our way, some of which are very good indeed. More interesting, perhaps, are the fortified liqueur Muscats of Rutherglen in Victoria (see also the 'Fortified Wines' sections on page 165).

**NEW ZEALAND**  It's great to think New Zealand's pure, citric sweet wines might become more readily available abroad in the future. Some of the Rieslings in particular, from wineries St. Clair and Ngatarawa, for example, are superb.

**REST OF THE WORLD**  And so on around the winemaking globe. Wherever dry table wine is taken seriously, there will be certain winemakers trying their hand at sweet versions. Perhaps the most fascinating left to mention is Vin de Constance, made by the Klein Constantia winery near Cape Town, South Africa. This lemony, fresh, prettily sweet wine is made from Muscat de Frontignan and recreates a legendary style supped regularly by the founders of the Cape wine trade centuries ago.

shortcuts to
success

# FIRST TASTE

• These wines are sweet, of course, but they are also very varied. Consider exactly how sweet an individual wine is. Does the acidity freshen up that sugariness and make for a well-balanced wine? Or are those sugar levels sickly and out of kilter?

• Look out for signs of botrytis (see pages 148–149). It's hard to describe, but generally botrytis adds richness and roundness, a hint of beeswax and overripe fruit, especially apricot.

• Try to spot the differences between dessert wines made from various grapes. Compare the classic Bordeaux blend of Sémillon and Sauvignon Blanc to the Chenin Blanc of the Loire, the Gewurztraminer of Alsace and the Rieslings from Germany, Austria and others. Which fruit flavours stand out? How high is the acidity and how viscous are the wines?

# BUYER'S GUIDE

• Sauternes can be divine, but it is horribly expensive. For better value, try sweet wines from other parts of the southwest Monbazillac, for example. They may not be quite as exciting and won't age so well, but they offer a snapshot of the style from this part of France.

• Sweet Muscats are heart-warmingly cheap, especially the Moscatels of Valencia and some of the fortified wines from southern France. They act as a good introduction to dessert wines: straightforward, honeyed, fresh and versatile with lots of puds.

• Look out for non-European stickies. More of them are appearing on our shop shelves as the import laws are loosened. They are reliably high in quality and reasonably priced.

# MOVING ON

• Fans of Bordeaux sweet wines should definitely make the Loire Valley their next vinous stop. The majestic, sweet Chenins of the Côteaux du Layon, Bonnezeaux and others are classics, and they'll cellar well for decades.

• Fine German botrytised Riesling is underrated by many. Make sure you swot up on the best sweet Rieslings and appreciate these superb wines.

• Try some of the pudding wines that are made in unusual ways – the *recioto* and vin santo wines of Italy, *Schilfweins* from the Neusiedler See in Austria. The world of dessert wines can be a strange one. There are lots of unusual and rare gems waiting to be discovered.

# fortified wines

Of all the styles, the fortified wines are the most difficult to pin down. Why? Well, they are so varied and extraordinary that they evade simple categorisation. How ironic, then, that for a lot of drinkers fortified wine equates to simple, warm, sticky sherry or port, consumed only at Christmas or with Great Auntie's Madeira cake on her birthday. Let me try to persuade you to re-think these classic and wonderful wines. Everyone should like fortified wine in at least one of its many different guises. Lovers of dry white wines will delight in a chilled glass of bone-dry fino sherry, one of the most mouth-watering aperitifs in the world. Those who dislike rich, red ports (some people will always associate them with hangovers) should attempt tawny port – mellow, nutty and soft – served lightly chilled with a homemade chocolate mousse.

Then there's Madeira, so often relegated to the kitchen cupboard and used only for cooking, but which can be magnificent, intense and intriguing. The fortified wines have so much concentrated flavour and aroma – it's partly why they are regularly used for sauces, of course – which is what makes them so fascinating and delicious. They are good value, too. A little goes a long way in the world of fortified wines and, once opened, they keep for longer than table wines (though not until next Christmas, please).

If you're bored with Chardonnay and Cabernet or if you find a lot of modern wines too one-dimensional and fruity (or, as some critics put it, tutti-frutti, conjuring up the fruit-salad-style of much new-wave wine), then here's your chance to experience some different sensations. These wines are laced with wild, heady, exotic nuances and have wonderful mouth-filling textures. They make for some truly fascinating food matches. Give them a go!

## APPEARANCE
More varied than many think. Sherry isn't only richly amber-coloured but ranges from very pale straw to deep mahogany. Port can be a bright garnet, a brown toffee colour, or dark purply-black. Madeira veers between pale and deep tawny.

## TEXTURE
Think thick. Most fortified wines have a gloopy, more viscous mouth-feel than ordinary table wines. This is because of higher alcohol levels, but also due to sweetness. The wine seems to fill your mouth; it's heavier and weightier than table wine.

# fortified wines

**AROMA** Most fortified wines are deeply aromatic. Expect fresh, tangy lemons, a whiff of fresh bread and yeast, even green olives in the case of dry fino and manzanilla sherries. Richer, sweeter fortifieds are often raisiny and caramelly in aroma. Look for hints of hazelnuts and dried citrus peel, too. Ports often have a red-cherry or fruitcake-like character or, in the case of tawny, they are very nutty.

**FLAVOUR** A wide spectrum of tasting notes, some straightforward, like lemons in fino and plums or cherries in red ports, but more exotic in others. Amontillado is distinctly nutty; oloroso is richly raisiny. Tawny port has a creamy, nut-oil flavour, while vintage port can be bursting with spice, damsons, chocolate, figs, and sloes. Also, expect rich, tough tannins in young vintage ports. Many fortified wines have a fresh, tangy, dry finish; others leave a sweet honeyed taste behind.

# Port

Port hails from Portugal, where it is made in the hot, arid Douro Valley to the north of the country. Here the vines cling to steep, rocky slopes either side of the wide river and yield small amounts of tannic, concentrated red. Don't expect to find a port made from well-known international grapes, such as Merlot or Cabernet. The vineyards in the Douro Valley are planted with a mixture of Portuguese varieties, including Touriga Nacional and Tinta Roriz, which bring unusual flavours to bear – wild herbs, tar, chocolate, fruitcake – as well as the usual red and black berry fruits.

All port is made in a similar way – at the beginning, that is. The grapes are crushed – sometimes by foot in traditional stone tanks called *lagares*, but usually by machine these days, and fermentation begins. This fermentation process is then effectively halted by the addition of grape spirit, which means any sugar that has not turned to alcohol remains in the liquid, hence the sweetness of port. At this point, the resulting liquid could go on to become one of two styles of port: ruby, or red, bottled fairly early and aged in glass; or tawny, which is placed into casks for long wood-ageing before bottling, so therefore takes on a more oaky character. Within these two categories there are several different types of port. Do try as many as you can (except the very basic ruby, which can be skipped) to grasp the range of port available and to get the right one for every occasion.

**VINTAGE PORT** Made from the wine of one fine year, vintage port is considered the most serious and complex of all ports. It is not made by each port shipper every year. Instead, connoisseurs have to wait with bated breath to see if a year has been considered good enough for a 'declaration' from their favourite house, in other words, an announcement that a vintage port will be made that year. On average a declaration is made three times a decade and, for obvious reasons, most houses declare in the same years when the conditions have been well above average. That said, there is the odd aberration. Cynics will point to declarations from houses that need a boost for some reason (perhaps it is a special anniversary year and it would seem a shame not to celebrate it). This method of sporadic declaration means stocks of the top vintage ports are strictly limited and prices remain high. It also follows that the quality should be pretty good for a universally declared vintage.

It's expensive stuff, then, in high demand, so what is so great about vintage port? It's bottled after just two years in cask and often seems unapproachable when young: tough with tannins, hard and unyielding, its fruit masked by sweetness, firm body and high acidity, elements which have not melded properly but stand apart. It often takes many years for a vintage port to seem well-knit and for its rich, plummy character to become appealing. When you choose to crack it open is up to your individual taste, of course. Most would agree that a serious vintage port only starts to loosen up and become drinkable at around ten years of age, and only softens to a truly delicious degree after fifteen, twenty or even thirty years. At that point expect a rich mouthful of fruitcake, black berry fruits, hints of herbs, tar, chocolate, mocha and spice.

Decant vintage port carefully before drinking, as it will have thrown a heavy sediment (see pages 174–175), and perhaps serve with the finest cheeses. Great port producers include Taylors, Dow, Warre, Graham, Niepoort and Noval. Recent top years include 2000, 1997, 1994, 1991, 1985, 1983, 1977, and 1970.

**SINGLE QUINTA PORT** This is vintage port from just one estate, or *quinta*, usually produced in years not considered fine enough for the regular flagship vintage port. The fruit from the single *quinta* often forms the backbone of the vintage port, so it may well make an excellent wine even in a less-than-perfect year. Single *quinta* ports tend to be not quite as rich and tannic as vintage ports, as they are made in lesser years, but they can be excellent value for money and offer you some of the joys of vintage port at a fraction of the price.

**LATE-BOTTLED VINTAGE**  Late-bottled vintage, or LBV, is usually another good-value port. It's made from a single year's wine, which spends five or six years ageing in wood casks. Still in a ruby style, LBVs are ready to drink earlier than vintage ports. The best are most impressive; however, a few are uninteresting and not much better than premium ruby. Choose carefully from a reputable producer (see those mentioned above) and don't cellar for long. LBVs may throw a sediment so pour the dregs carefully or decant.

**RUBY**  A port labelled as ruby is usually a cheapish wine bottled after two or three years in a large oak cask. It can be attractive for its youthful, lively, cherryish fruit attack. Drink it unmixed while fresh and young, but never keep a bottle, opened or unopened, for too long. 'Premium ruby' and 'vintage character port' are supposedly superior rubies; they are, generally speaking, a little more concentrated and interesting than basic ruby. A decent ruby is best served at room temperature on a cold winter's evening to put fire in your belly. Graham's Six Grapes is one of the best premium rubies.

**TAWNY**  Tawny port is quite a different creature to the ruby, or red, port styles. It is aged in oak for many years until it evolves into a soft, rounded, amber-coloured port with a hazelnut and sometimes lightly spiced character. You can buy ten-, twenty-, thirty- and forty-year-old tawnies; it is well worth buying one that is at least twenty years old for its extra-mellow and intensely nutty quality. Ramos-Pinto, Fonseca and Sandeman are names to go for.

## Storing and serving

It's a myth that, once opened, all fortified wines keep perfectly well for years in the drinks cabinet. If you want to enjoy them at their best, most fortifieds need drinking up within two to three weeks. Dry, pale sherries should be finished within a week or two at the most. Madeira is an exception, however, as it keeps for months once opened. Unopened bottles of fortified wine do keep for several months, except dry, pale sherries that need drinking when young and fresh. Vintage port is released young for you to age; cellar for many years before opening.

# Sherry

Sherry is made in Andalucía, southern Spain, in and around three towns: Jerez, Sanlúcar de Barrameda and El Puerto de Santa María. It's produced predominantly from Palomino grapes growing on chalky, white soil known as *albariza*. The uninspiring, neutral, base wine made from these grapes is placed in oak butts… then something exciting happens. The wine is affected by the natural yeast in the air, forming a thick, creamy blanket, called *flor*, on the surface. This protects the wine from oxidation while at the same time giving it a characteristic ripe, yeasty, bready quality. The result is dry, tangy sherry. Other sherry styles, as we shall see, emerge in slightly different ways.

Sherry sales seem to be moving up at last, following a long period during which this wonderful classic Spanish wine was considered old-fashioned and boring. Thank goodness we are enjoying sherry again; it can be one of the greatest wines in the world and extremely well-priced. Most people think of sweet, dark, cream sherry first and foremost, yet more and more of us are discovering the delights of dry sherry, if not the full spectrum of styles from mouth-watering manzanilla to the amazingly concentrated and deeply luscious Pedro Ximénez, or PX. Sherry is even more varied than port, so to understand it fully you really need to sample various different types. As sherry doesn't keep particularly long once opened, especially the dry styles, try buying half-bottles.

One or two more salient facts. Sherry is made only in Andalucía, in southern Spain (the name 'sherry' comes from Jerez, one of the three sherry-producing towns). Since the early nineties no other fortified wine has been allowed to use the word 'sherry' on its label. So, when you buy a wine labelled 'sherry', it's the real McCoy rather than some cheap, dull imitation from another country (this is now labelled 'fortified wine'). The pale styles, both dry and sweet, are best served chilled, when fresh from a young bottle. Always avoid a dusty vessel that has been sitting on a shop shelf for months. Sherry is perhaps not as strong as you think, fortified to anything between fifteen and a half percent and twenty percent. (Compare this with a typical southern-hemisphere table wine at around fourteen percent.)

Finally, although one or two great sherry producers simply must be tried, don't avoid cheaper supermarket sherries for everyday drinking as the general standard is excellent.

**FINO AND MANZANILLA**  Fino is made from the first pressings of Palomino grapes, which are affected by *flor*. It tastes so dry and tangy, it's almost salty. Expect lemons, green olives and yeasty, doughy hints. Serve as a cold, palate-freshening aperitif with snacks such as crisps, olives, prawns and nuts. Manzanilla is the name given to exactly the same style of sherry, but made in the coastal town of Sanlúcar de Barrameda. If anything, it's yeastier, breadier and slightly softer. Brands of both to try include Hidalgo's La Gitana, Barbadillo's Solear, Domecq's La Iña, and González Byass' Tío Pepe.

**AMONTILLADO AND DRY OLOROSO**
Amontillado sherry starts off as a fino, but is then fortified to around seventeen or eighteen percent, killing off the flor and exposing the wine to the air. The wine then oxidises, giving a nutty quality and a darker amber colour. It's a medium sherry, perfect with a meaty consommé, but the quality of amontillado varies somewhat. Choose a good brand, such as González Byass's dry Del Duque or Valdespiño's Tío Diego. Dry oloroso (meaning aromatic) is often cited as the most intriguing of sherries – rich and raisiny, but with a savoury, lip-smacking finish. Try a dry oloroso from the Lustau or Valdespiño ranges served with fine cheese.

## Matching fortified wines with food

Don't save fortified wines for after dinner or to sip by the fire at Christmas; they make great partners for food, too. Fino and manzanilla are perfect for washing down salty snacks, such as olives, anchovies and crisps, or try them with seafood and even sushi. Sweet cream sherry is a superb partner for mince pies or bread-and-butter pudding. Dry oloroso and vintage port are fine with cheese, while aged tawny port is heavenly with chocolate or a handful of nuts. Australian liqueur Muscat is superb with toffee-flavoured puddings. Verdelho Madeira is a classic match for consommé. And so on… Try some unusual food and fortified matches yourself.

## Making the difference

The *solera* system, used to produce sherry and Montilla, is a complex way of blending young and old wines from a series of barrels of different ages, stacked together in layers. As sherry is drawn out of the bottom cask, so it is topped up from the barrel above, which in turn is replenished from the one above that. As some *solera* systems are decades or even centuries old, small fractions of ancient sherry end up in the finished wine.

**SWEET SHERRIES** The best sweet and cream sherries contain good-quality oloroso wine; the worst are unbalanced and sickly. Pale cream, which is a light straw colour but delicately sweet, can be delectable served straight from the fridge with fresh fruit desserts. Richer cream, such as Harvey's Bristol Cream, is served at room temperature with mince pies or luxury cakes. Pedro Ximénez, or PX, is a rarer wine made from the grape of the same name. It is ludicrously thick and unctuous with the flavour of intensely sweet treacle and raisins. PX is great with ginger cake or even poured over vanilla ice-cream!

# Madeira

Despite the common perception of it as old-fashioned – the Duke of Clarence drowning in a butt of Malmsey is still a potent image – Madeira remains a lovely, venerable drink that is well worth trying. If you don't like it, it can always be used in cooking, but I guarantee that if you pick a good one, you will be surprised by the complexity and drinkability of this mellow fortified wine.

Made on the Portuguese island of the same name, quality Madeira is produced from four noble grapes: Sercial, Verdelho, Bual and Malmsey. Respectively, these make dry, medium, medium-sweet and very sweet, figgy wines. During the production process, Madeira is heated to give it burnt-caramel undertones. A consequence of this is that it keeps for a remarkably long time – for months once opened, but for decades or even centuries unopened. It should have quite high acidity and a tangy note on the finish. Serve dry styles chilled as aperitif wines; medium styles with soups, Bual with cheeses and Malmsey with desserts. Cheaper Madeiras (no grape is named on the label) are made from the lesser Tinta Negra Mole; these can be palatable, though not nearly as complex or long-lived as those made from noble grapes. Best of all are the noble Madeiras – the grape is named on the label – aged for ten years or more (this age appears on the label, too). Blandy, Cossart-Gordon and Henriques & Henriques are brands to go for.

# Other fortified wines

**MONTILLA** Montilla is sherry-like wine made mainly from PX grapes in the Spanish hills south of Córdoba (see pages 163–165). Some wines are fortifed, others are not. Most Montilla sold on export is sweet, simple stuff. Go to Córdoba, however, and you may get to try the superior aged oloroso styles.

**MARSALA** Marsala is a sweet fortified wine made in Sicily, where regulations allow for it to be sweetened. It is distinctly toffeed and nutty. Choose a good producer such as de Bartoli or Pelligrino.

**MUSCATS** Australian liqueur Muscats have been described as 'liquid Christmas pudding' and indeed are dark, richly raisined and alcoholic. Some taste distinctly of dates, while others are chocolatey. They are made in the state of Victoria, around the town of Rutherglen. The best brands include Campbells, Stanton & Killeen and Yalumba. Some fortified sweet French Muscats – strictly pudding wines – are dealt with in the section on 'Sweet Wines' on page 149.

# FIRST TASTE

• Smell your fortified wine carefully before you drink it. The strong aroma is essential to the pleasure of the wine. Look for unusual and exotic nuances on the perfume.

• Sample dry as well as sweet styles of sherry and Madeira. Most associate these wines with sweetness, but some bone-dry examples are out there and they are delicious.

• Pick the right moments to try various types of fortified wine. They are not all at their best at Christmas. For example, chilled fino sherry makes a brilliant summer aperitif and tawny port goes well with cold puddings, such as chocolate or coffee mousse.

# BUYER'S GUIDE

• Cheaper sherries are worth a try; there are even some decent supermarket own-label sherries out there. Give them a go if you're on a tight budget.

• Avoid very inexpensive ruby port. If you can't manage vintage, try to buy LBV and single-quinta port, as these offer good value for money.

• Consider buying half-bottles. That way you open a fresh bottle of fortified wine more frequently and don't have dusty, old, unfinished bottles lying around for months.

• Madeira is divided into the more affordable and more mundane stuff. Go for aged Madeiras, five-year-old, ten-year-old and twenty-year-old, made from the noble grapes – Sercial, Verdelho, Bual and Malmsey – named on the label rather than that made from Tinta Negra Mole grapes.

# MOVING ON

• Try more unusual styles of port and sherry, including white port, crusted port, Palo Cortado and PX sherry. These will make more sense if you have tried the common types, so are not for beginners.

• Attempt some interesting food matching. Try fino sherry with sushi, PX sherry with raisins soaked in it, and Sercial Madeira with salted almonds.

• Buy a case of vintage port and lay it down for ageing. After ten years or so, open a bottle each year to see how it evolves over time.

# 3 the know-how

# storing wine

The vast majority of the bottles we buy are cracked open and enjoyed within twenty-four days of purchase – despite all you hear about cellaring or 'laying down' wine, few of us actually do it. There's nothing wrong with this 'drink 'em quick' attitude. Many reds produced today are deliberately created in an easygoing, soft and smooth style which makes for delicious early enjoyment. And a high number of fairly simple, light, dry whites, rosés and sparklers should be opened while young or they lose their fresh appeal.

But most of us have the odd bottle lying around – something a bit special, perhaps, or a wine that we are saving for a particular occasion. You don't need a serious storage plan to keep a few bottles for a week or two, obviously, but do think about where and how you put them if they are hanging around for more than a few days. Above all, keep your wine in a cool, dark spot – this fragile liquid suffers if it is stored in a hot place (or, worse, a place where temperatures fluctuate a lot), or if it is kept in direct sunlight. I'm especially bothered by the latest trend for mini-wine racks placed near the oven – often a feature of the modern fitted kitchen. The kitchen is not an ideal room for wine at all as it gets much too hot in there, nearly every day. Wine stored in warm, sunny places quickly loses its fresh fruitiness, so don't leave it on the windowsill in high summer, either!

## Makeshift cellars

Instead, buy a huge multi-millionaire's house with a big cellar, fitted with state-of-the-art wine racks. Only kidding! There are plenty of places in the ordinary home where wine can be kept safely and sensibly. The cupboard under the stairs is usually a good bet – make sure you don't store any white spirits or pungent paints down there as well, since there's some evidence that wine can be affected by strong-smelling substances. Lay the bottles on their sides if you are keeping them for more than a couple of weeks. This stops the cork from drying out – a shrivelled-up cork can let air in to the bottle and spoil the wine. If you invest in a small wine rack, go for a wooden one as metal racks can easily tear the labels when the bottles are removed.

Alternative spots for storing a few bottles include: at the bottom of a wardrobe, in a downstairs cloakroom, under the spare bed… anywhere, really, where it stays relatively cool and dark and where you are not likely to disturb your bottles and break them. The garage is not a great idea, as it can get very cold, and often has petrol and paint fumes. Some people worry about leaving white and sparkling wine in the fridge for any length of time. There's nothing wrong with storing an everyday bottle in there for a day or two, but watch out it isn't too cold when you serve it, as a serious chill can mute the flavour and aroma of wine. Thaw it out a bit before opening.

## Professional wine storage

What if you are developing a real passion for wine and want to start a serious collection? A cellar *is* the best storage option; it tends to be cooler and darker and sometimes a little humid down below: perfect conditions for wine. If you are lucky enough to have a cellar in your house, empty it of all smelly substances, but don't repaint it or wash it down with lots of cleaning fluid – wine doesn't mind a bit of dirt but it may be affected by chemicals in the air. Line a wall or two with decent racks and buy some cellar tags for putting over the necks of your bottles to help you identify them. It's possible to keep wine in its original case, as well as on a rack; as long as the bottles are lying on their sides and can't break, they will be fine. It may be worth keeping a 'cellar book' to record when you opened the wine and what it tasted like – especially if you have lots of the same bottles stored there, as you can chart that wine's development easily.

## Other storage options

Of course there are wine buffs who lack cellars, but have built up an impressive collection nonetheless. One option is a temperature-controlled unit that looks just like a fridge, but is filled with racks and designed to keep fine wine in exactly the right conditions. These are expensive (expect to splash out at least £750) but cheaper than moving, of course, and may be worth the investment if you are embarking on a lifetime of fine-wine collecting. Even more pricey are the spiral-shaped cellars that are bored into the ground floor of your home (the door is hidden under a rug in the living room or kitchen, for example). These cost nearer £5,000– £10,000 but are impressive: a small circular underground cellar is created, lined with wine racks and with a central staircase to provide access. One of these may add some value onto your home, of course. Flat owners need not apply…

Most of us find some solution to the problem. We don't have a cellar in our country cottage but we have a reasonable collection of fine wine, which lives in a cool, walk-in cupboard off the hall which the previous owner used as a 'gun' room. I know a wine-crazy Londoner who keeps his loot in the outside loo, at the bottom of his garden, with a thermostat controlling the temperature. Others keep their collection with a wine storage specialist.

## Wines worth hanging on to

As mentioned above, most ordinary, inexpensive wine is meant to be consumed soon after you buy it. That goes for soft, light, 'everyday' reds as well as dry whites. As a rule of thumb, the lighter and less substantial the wine (think Pinot Grigio, Muscadet, basic Beaujolais, cheap fizz), the more quickly you must open it. Richer 'everyday' wines (non-European Chardonnay, Cab-Shiraz blends, ordinary Rhône reds)

last a bit longer unopened – up to a year after purchase, before starting to lose their vibrant flavours and aromas. Note that red Rioja, even a very expensive label, is aged at the winery in Spain and released ready to drink. Likewise LBV (late-bottled vintage) and tawny ports. Don't be tempted to store them for long.

But some wines are supposed to be kept – they actually taste better if you lay them down for a period. Among these are young, tough premium reds from Bordeaux (claret); vintage Champagnes; fine German Rieslings, both sweet and dry (and similar bottles from Austria); rich, tannic Cabernets and Cabernet blends from the southern hemisphere; top Australian Semillons; top-of-the-range Rhône reds; Barolos, Barbarescos and Amarones from Italy; the great French dessert wines from Sauternes and best Loire Valley whites. These wines will all benefit from some bottle-age (assuming you buy recent vintages), becoming more mellow, their acidity softer, their flavours more well-knit, with honeyed undertones in the whites and smoother, earthier, even gamey notes in the reds.

It's obviously a matter of taste whether you like mature wines or youthful ones. In the case of certain styles, like red burgundy, there is something to be said for the bright, red-fruit character of the younger wines and the truffley, horsey, richly gamey character of older ones. Both are valid. In the UK, fine wines were traditionally drunk when they were very mature (the French were often shocked by this and rather sniffily called it *le goût Anglais*, 'the English taste'.) Now younger wines are preferred with more fresh-fruit flavours. As with so many things in the world of wine, work out which suits you best. A serious collection should give you ample opportunity to try out wines both young and old!

## Wine accessories

The passionate wine buff might wish to own a whole host of wine accessories; fancy pieces of kit that should be there to help with the process of serving and enjoying wine, but which are probably there only to impress! From the drip-stop silver collar, to the wine thermometer, to the pewter coaster, these collectables are only useful to a degree, and if truth be told, you can get by fine without recourse to any of them. One of the most useful, in my view, is the humble, inexpensive chiller sleeve, a frozen plastic 'arm-band' which chills wine adequately well in a matter of minutes. As I have explained opposite, a decanter is a good idea, but to be honest, a good glass jug will suffice. Own these two items, plus a good corkscrew (the cheap waiter's friend, lever-style model is fine), and you don't really need anything else. Except the wine, of course!

# serving table wines

Is it just me, or are certain bottles of wine sometimes very difficult to get into? Natural corks seem to get stuck with annoying frequency and I have to call on a strong man (okay, my husband) to get them out. Plastic stoppers, which are sometimes made to look just like bark corks, are easier in this respect, but tend to be difficult to pull off the corkscrew! Perhaps these are two further reasons why the screwcap is making a such a comeback – it's not just about combating cork taint. However, the following tips should help you get into any bottle, whether it has a natural or a plastic cork.

Buy a not-very-expensive, simple, lever-type corkscrew called a waiter's friend. (Waiters keep them in their pockets.) Once mastered, it's hard to beat a waiter's friend, even with a fancy designer corkscrew. Screw it in, then use the ledge on the side of the handle to push against the bottle as you slowly and steadily lever the cork out. This is not so good with modern bottles that have flattened, wide rims (flange tops); indeed, these are the most difficult wines to open without chipping the glass neck, so if opening ain't your strong point, steer clear of the flange design fad.

Here's how to serve wine well. Remove any bits of cork crumble around the lip of the bottle, simply because they will look bad in a glass (they don't affect the flavour). Then slowly pour the wine into the glass, filling it only about one-third of the way up. This doesn't mean you are stingy, but it lets you swirl the liquid around, and savour its appearance and aroma. Do what the experts do – fill it up frequently, but never right to the top (unless it's a Champagne flute, which looks odd half empty). This is helpful for keeping whites cold, too, as it means the wine can stay in the bottle in a cool spot, rather than sitting around warming up in your glass.

Pour rich reds, especially older ones, and fine vintage ports with great care. They may have a sediment that has collected in the bottom of the bottle over the years (or along its side if it has been in a rack). No one wants to sip a mouthful of black gunk, so remove the sediment by decanting the bottle gradually and cautiously into a glass decanter (or a clean jug), and stop as soon as you see the sediment start to appear in the liquid. Chuck away the dregs.

It's also worth decanting rich, tannic reds which *don't* have a sediment, as exposure to the air mellows them and helps their aroma and flavour to emerge. Forget messing around opening the bottle half an hour before dinner; it won't have a great effect on the liquid. Instead, decant the wine into another container, as above, or even pour it into big-bowled glasses and swoosh it around firmly to aerate at the table.

The ideal wineglass is neither a pricey, multi-faceted crystal one nor a modern, brightly coloured one. To see your wine properly, go for plain glass, and choose a thin one, as that feels much nicer on the mouth than chunky, thick glass does and is more elegant all round. Pick glasses with long stems, so you can hold the glass there, rather than wrapping your fingers round the bowl and warming up the wine. And go for a fairly big bowl so you can swirl the wine effectively and release its aroma. Serve sherry and port from ordinary white-wine glasses – throw those old-fashioned little schooners away! The Austrian company Riedel makes some of the best glasses in the world and many wine fans seek them out.

# serving sparkling wines

The age-old problem of how to open sparkling wine seems to defeat many, including Formula One drivers. There is a technique to this, however, and once mastered, you will be amazed how simple it seems. This is why waiters almost always impress when they open a bottle of fizz; it looks as though there is a secret to it, but they are simply following a few guidelines.

Of course, shaking the bottle vigorously and popping it open suddenly is the worst thing to do, especially if it's a Champagne that cost a fortune. Bubbly is under enormous pressure, so if you don't open it slowly and carefully, the cork could explode from the bottle, wasting your fizz, and possibly putting someone's eye out. I'm not joking – opening sparkling wine and Champagne can be dangerous – so make sure the bottle isn't pointing at anyone. It's best to aim up at the point where the wall meets the ceiling. Hold the bottle at an angle as it is less likely to fizz up and out in a rush. It's also worth knowing that chilled fizz is less explosive than warmer stuff.

The best way to get to your bubbly is to hold the base of the bottle firmly in one hand (use a dry tea-towel to grip it if damp), and with the other hand, undo the foil wrap and the wire cage. As you take the wire cage off, keep a couple of fingers hovering over the cork, prepared to contain an explosion at any point. Then gently, slowly, twist the bottle one way, and the cork the other, aiming to prise it out gradually. The result is a soft, satisfying hiss as the cork is released into your hand, and very little fizz, if any, should be lost.

Serve in tall, elegant flutes, preferably with plain bowls so that you can see the pretty colour of the wine and the tiny streams of bubbles rising through the liquid. Fill right up (flutes don't suit being half full, and anyway, it's hard to swirl fizz) and pour gently, holding the glass at an angle so the liquid doesn't froth too much and overflow.

## Champagne glasses

The traditional wide, shallow-bowled Champagne glasses (said to have been made in honour of Marie-Antoinette's breasts) look luxurious, but they have fallen out of fashion in favour of tall flutes. This is partly because the bubbles in sparkling wine dissipate more quickly in wide bowls – there is simply more surface area for them to pop up to. Flat fizz isn't the idea at all, so many people now prefer flutes, which seem to retain the sparkle more effectively.

# detecting faults in wine

It doesn't pay to be a wimp if you think your wine is faulty. Many of us are severely embarrassed about complaining and shy away from it, when we are quite comfortable making a fuss about poor food, bad clothes or rip-off holidays. I'll let you in on a well-kept secret that some of the wine trade want to keep hidden: there is *no* special mystery about faulty wine.

If you don't like a wine for some reason, take it back to the shop or send it back if you are in a restaurant. You do not have to understand the problem like a top-ranking merchant or wine waiter does. Just explain that the wine tastes of vinegar, or smells musty, or appears to be cloudy or so on. As long as you haven't drained the bottle (that would be taking the mick) you can expect to receive a replacement – either a new bottle of the same wine or a similarly priced one.

There is one proviso when returning wine, however: try not to complain that the wine is not the style you like. There's a big difference between a faulty wine and one that doesn't suit you. A kind retailer might replace a wine bought in error, but not everyone will. Restaurants are especially snooty about this.

If you keep buying the wrong sort of wine, make sure you ask more questions about a bottle before you buy it, or read this book carefully before you go shopping. You can't expect to take back an extremely cheap white, say, just because it is a bit boring, or a bargain-basement red because it is a touch over-oaky. No, we're talking faults here: nasty, bitter, acidic, over-sweet, mouldy, flabby, oxidised wine. No one should pay good money for something that tastes truly revolting!

The most prevalent wine fault is caused by cork taint. Corked wine has nothing to do with a crumbling cork. It means that a mould-affected cork has spoilt the wine, giving a musty aroma and cardboard flavour (think damp cardboard, old kitchen clothes, even

mushrooms). This trait can be quite pronounced in some wines, but disarmingly subtle in others, sometimes just deadening the fresh-fruit aroma and taste of the wine. Corked wine gets worse the longer it is opened, so wait awhile if you are not sure and try it again. If you suspect the wine is corked (you can't prove it and shouldn't have to) take or send it back and demand a replacement.

Despite some efforts on the part of the cork industry, the number of corked bottles remains unacceptably high – some estimates put it as one in eight bottles, although one in twelve is my reckoning – and this is why plastic corks and screwcaps are sometimes used instead. The use of screwcaps for premium wines, especially in New Zealand and Australia, is on the rise.

Other faults to look out for include oxidised wine (where the air has got in and spoilt it – much as an apple turns brown once chopped), wine with 'foreign objects' in it (I found tiny fruit flies on one memorable occasion), and heavily sulphured wine. Sulphur is used as a preservative when most wines are bottled, but overuse of it leads to a wine which smells of struck matches, and may cause problems to asthma sufferers and others allergic to this chemical. The stricter regulations for organic wine mean it usually contains much less sulphur. Send stinking sulphurous wines back!

Don't worry about wine that has thrown a natural sediment, however (see page 171 for more on this) or ones with little white crystals in the bottle. The latter are harmless tartrate deposits and don't affect the taste of your wine.

# using up leftover wine

Drinking up time! There's a tendency to hang on to leftover wine for too long. Once the cork is pulled on a bottle, air gets to the liquid and the wine starts to oxidise and deteriorate – fast. You just can't leave opened bottles standing around for weeks and expect the wine to remain delicious.

This is as true of expensive, fine wines as it is of cheap-and-cheerful ones. After the first serving, stick the cork back in the bottle, and store it in a cool, dark place (the fridge, if it is a wine that suits being chilled). Drink up table wines within two days if they are soft, light styles, and within three if they are rich and full-bodied. Mature wines seem to deteriorate more quickly than youthful, tannic ones. A superb, but fragile, old red burgundy can fall apart in a couple of hours, as I once witnessed in a restaurant. It was hard to say who was more shocked, the distinctly upper-crust waiter, me, or my friend, who was paying!

Sherry is hopelessly abused by being kept for months, even years, after it is opened. Dry, pale sherries (finos and manzanillas) should be treated just like a white wine – opened when young, served fresh and cold from the fridge, and ditched after a few days if unfinished. Richer styles last a little longer but don't keep any sherry for more than three weeks. Port doesn't like living in a drinks cabinet for months, either – simple ruby and tawny need drinking within a week of opening, while fuller styles can last for two.

A lot of nonsense is talked about keeping the fizz in sparkling wine. There are various techniques that make a few bubbles last a day or two, including a special cap that clamps down on the bottle, but frankly, the wine is never quite the same as when it is first opened. Drink it up, I say, or get more friends round next time! Some people swear by special wine-preservation products; these either pump most of the air out of the bottle, leaving a vacuum which is then sealed, or they coat the liquid left inside with a layer of gas to stop it oxidising. It's true that they lengthen the life of still wine by a few days, but to be honest, I can never be bothered with them, and prefer to switch to half-bottles if our wine intake is going to be low.

## Cooking with wine

So what do you do with any leftovers? Most of us have a nearly empty bottle lurking somewhere in the kitchen, collecting dust and looking a bit sad. If it's ancient, ditch it. If it's only a week or so old, you can use it in a cooking – to add flavour to a meat casserole, for example, or to bolognese sauce if it's red. Whites kept in the fridge for the same length of time might be used to make sauces for fish and chicken or vegetable bakes. Make sure it's not a heavily oaked style of white, however, as an overtly oaky flavour doesn't taste right in food. Avoid using warmer-climate Chardonnay, white Rioja and rich white burgundy in the kitchen for this reason.

The best grape for sauces, adding a bit of tanginess and a light appley flavour, is probably Riesling. Leftover sparkling wine and Champagne also adds something fresh and tasty to white sauces – even when the fizz has gone. Rosé (and sparkling rosé) also makes a pleasant, red-berryish, fruity addition to sauces and lighter (say, chicken) stews.

Here are some more ideas – not just for leftovers, but for cooking with wine in general:

• Madeira is seen as a staple of the kitchen store cupboard because it doesn't go off in the bottle for months (even years) after opening, and because it adds a lovely, rich nuttiness to sauces. Use it to deglaze a pan after cooking red meat and pour the juices over the dish. By the way, Madeira is a great drink, not just a useful cooking ingredient.

• Make lemon sorbet with the addition of a little Champagne (or, more frugally, with cava – it will taste almost as good). Pink sparkling wine can be used for a delicate red-berry sorbet. Decide whether you want to use dry fizz (*brut* on the label) or a sweeter style (*demi-sec*) as this will affect the final dish.

• Dump the dregs from a decanted bottle of serious red wine or port into a hearty stew – they will add a little character, body and flavour. Honest!

• Poach pears (and other fruit) in sweet wine – don't squander your best Sauternes in this way, obviously, but try an inexpensive, but attractive and honeyed Moscatel from Valencia, or a French Muscat. If you are going to poach fruit in red wine, make it a soft, ripe, fruity red – not a heavy, tannic, oaky one.

• Add a splash of port to rich stews. Use a fairly cheap ruby port for an extra dab of fruity flavour.

• Cook with the same sort of wine that you intend to drink with the dish – Rhône red in the sauce and in the glass, for example. You could try a cheaper one in the sauce than at the table, but do keep to similar styles, as the food and wine will chime in well together.

• A last word of warning: don't use extremely cheap, nasty wine for cooking. That horrible bottle you simply couldn't bear to sip, or that plastic jug of plonk brought back from France should go nowhere near your finest fare. I'm not suggesting you use pricey, premium wine for cooking, but avoid anything that tastes unpleasant in the glass – a little bit of that unpleasantness will show up in the food. Truly grim wine belongs down the plughole!

# matching wine with food

Throughout Part Two of this book, there are plenty of tips for successful wine and food matching. These are only meant as suggestions; if you enjoy a full-bodied Australian Shiraz with prawn cocktail, or a delicate Italian white with your steak, then go right ahead. There are no hard-and-fast rules about the marriage between wine and food these days, so don't let a wine snob tell you otherwise.

Anyone who travels a lot will discover various combinations which might be considered appalling in the UK are quite normal in other parts of the world. The Portuguese like to drink rich reds with *bacalhau* (salt cod) for example, while Argentinians think nothing of pairing dry red Malbec and chocolate cake – both these pairings work surprisingly well, by the way.

Although we are released from the strictures of traditional food and wine matching, it does help to follow some basic guidelines when you are trying to achieve the perfect marriage. And it is worth trying hard to get it right; certain combinations of food and wine are sublime, somehow enhancing each other and bringing certain flavours to the fore. Aim for a careful balance above all else – the very reason Portuguese red wine goes with salt cod is that this particular form of fish is so meaty and rich.

Big food needs big wine. Light food requires light wine, acidic ingredients need acidic wines, heavy meats go with tannic wines, sweetness in the food calls for sweet notes in the wine. If one or other element outweighs the other, the match won't work. So don't try 'lifting' a blockbuster main course by serving an elegant, restrained wine with it – the food will walk all over the wine and you won't taste what's in your glass. Likewise, don't put a mega-oaky, fruit-driven Aussie Chardonnay with a leafy salad and seafood, as your meal will be utterly overpowered by the flavours in your glass. Match like with like.

Bear in mind all the ingredients in a dish when choosing a wine to go with it. It may be a chicken recipe, but how is the chicken cooked? If it's in a lemon sauce, you'll need a medium-bodied white; if it's in a red wine and onion stew, then try a red, or if it's roast chicken with all the trimmings, a red or a white may do, as long as they are both soft and richly fruity. Add various condiments, relishes and sauces and you may need to think all over again.

Try to match sweetness levels in both food and wine. This applies not only to desserts – very sweet, luscious wines with luxuriously rich puds, but lightly honeyed, tarter wines with fresh fruit – but also to savoury dishes which have a succulent hint of sweetness. Some seafood (crab, lobster, scallops) and certain meat dishes (duck, ham, pork) have an inherent sweetness, as do root vegetables. They may be better off with a medium-dry wine than a bone-dry one. Try off-dry Rieslings or Loire whites, perhaps.

Notice the number of regional marriages that work – in certain parts of France and Italy, the food and the wine really do seem well-suited. They have grown up and evolved side by side, so it stands to reason that they often taste good together.

Finally, think about the sauces and trimmings that suit a dish, and try to echo these flavours in a wine. Lemon goes well with fish and seafood, and so do lemony wines; redcurrant jelly is delicious with lamb, and so are wines which taste of red berries (and indeed, ones which taste of mint, as in certain Cabernet Sauvignons); meaty stews suit a twist of black pepper and, surprise! the peppery Syrah/Shiraz grape makes a fine partner for them. And so on. Matching food and wine is great fun, so experiment to your heart's content.

# restaurant wines

I have already suggested we are too reticent over complaining about faulty wines; now here's another area where we could do with a lot more confidence: ordering wine in restaurants. There we are, the diners, willing to fork out for often horribly marked-up fine wines, and for some reason we feel nervous about it and reluctant to ask many questions of the waiter.

It's important to trade up from restaurant house wines, as many are substandard. House wines are supposed to be the favourite bottles for everyday tippling as chosen by the restaurant owner. In some cases, that's exactly what they are, but often they are fobbed off on a customer by a restaurant, who in turn was fobbed off by a wine merchant needing to off-load some cheap plonk. If you do want a house wine, try it before ordering a bottle, unless it's a wine you know well.

When ordering restaurant wines, don't sweat! Make the staff do all the hard work. Ask your sommelier (wine waiter) lots of questions about the wines on the list, get him/her to describe them and help you to pick a good vintage and a bottle that suits your food. Be cheeky and ask for a taste before you buy (there may be a bottle open). If you're still in doubt, order one glass before committing to a bottle – the restaurant may oblige even if it isn't normally offered by the glass.

If the wine is in any way bad send it back without a second's thought. The waiter should replace a faulty wine without question. They should also provide iced buckets/coolers for chilled wine, offer you a peek at the bottle before opening (check the vintage is correct) and a taste before pouring, then top your glass up regularly or leave the bottle where you can reach it.

A decent wine list should assist rather than hinder your choice with not only the range of wines available, but also the words on the page. Wines listed should carry brief, user-friendly tasting notes and some food matches, and the region, producer and vintage should all be there, too. There are plenty of lists that say 'Sancerre' or 'Cabernet-Shiraz' followed only by the price, which simply isn't good enough. Over to the wine waiter, then, for more information!

I once asked for the wine list in a restaurant to be handed a card that simply said 'red' on one side and 'white' on the other. Those were the only options: a solitary red or a solitary white. I suppose it was a satirical comment on the fact that so many wine lists today seem to run on and on, taking in hundreds of bin numbers. We drank beer that night, as I didn't trust the jokers to provide palatable plonk. But the point was made – endless columns of many different wines can be off-putting and confusing. When you have gone out to eat and relax, should you be made to read a huge tome of wine suggestions? It seems too much like hard work. Here's how to tackle it…

If you are presented with a multitude of wines to choose from, look for a shorter list at the front or back. Many top restaurants offer a slate of, say, twenty-five wines to save you going through the main list of five hundred. No? Then take a close look at the format of the long list, particularly how the wines are grouped. In the past, lists were divided by country and region, but today some restaurants choose to group the wines by style or grape variety. These groupings can be very useful, so rather than simply sticking a pin in anywhere, use the way the information is presented to guide you. The best lists offer tasting notes and some even suggest matches for specific dishes on the menu. Again, use this information to your advantage.

One last tip. Don't ignore the nooks and crannies of a wine list, where the more unusual wines may lurk. Interesting aperitifs offered in good restaurants (but rarely taken up) include dry sherry and sparklers, such as non-European fizz, Prosecco and vintage cava, by the glass. Wonderful ways to finish a feast are a small glass of dessert wine, port, sweet sherry or Madeira. Rather than buying one bottle to see you both through dinner, why not each buy three glasses of quite different wines at various stages of the meal? That's exactly the way the wonderful world of wine starts to open up…

When choosing your wine, consider all the main ingredients of what you are eating (not just the chicken or fish). Bear in mind that some wines are more food-friendly than others. An ancient bottle of gamey, leathery burgundy might make the perfect partner for one particular dish – say, roast pheasant – but it won't necessarily go with anything else ordered and may well clash horribly with some choices. But a bottle of Chianti Classico will suit most meat dishes found on a menu and should go nicely with robust vegetarian food and cheese as well. Chianti isn't necessarily a better wine, but if several of you are matching dishes, it is more versatile, being medium-bodied and well-balanced.

Other wines that suit a wide range of dishes, and so are perfect for ordering for more than one in restaurants, are the appley Pinot Blanc grape (from Alsace, in particular), French Sauvignon Blanc and Sauvignon-Sémillon blends (white Bordeaux), unoaked or lightly oaked Chardonnay, young Pinot Noir, Chilean Merlot, Australian Cabernet-Shiraz, Rioja *reserva*, Chianti, southern Italian reds and Argentinian Malbec.

The following is a (very) general guide to a big evening out for four people with a very long wine list. Incidentally, keep the list with you throughout the meal – waiters are usually far too keen to prise it off you – but don't read it all evening! This is supposed to help keep your studies to a minimum.

• On arrival, ask for the wine and turn to the sections on sparkling wine or Champagne, dry fino or manzanilla sherry, or the lightest dry white wines. Unless you are a big party, order aperitifs by the glass.

• While you peruse the menu and choose your food, look for a 'short section' to the wine list. If there is none, work out how the list is ordered and check for tasting notes and food matches. Order a bottle of light, dry white; in nearly all cases, it will go down well with at least some of the starters and even the odd main course. Definitely choose one if fish, seafood, vegetarian food or light, spicy dishes are being ordered. Try a fine Riesling (German, Alsatian, Austrian or non-European), a Sauvignon Blanc (Sancerre or Pouilly-Fumé or a New Zealand or South African example), or a lighter white from southwest France (Entre-Deux-Mers, perhaps). I guarantee it will go down well during the first half of the meal.

• If richer fish or poultry is being ordered, look at the richer whites, including Chardonnay (white burgundy or non-European examples), Albariño, Sémillon or Viognier. Consider whether the dishes will go well with an oaky white. A serious, powerful Chardonnay from California or Australia might please those who order roast chicken or fresh salmon. But only order such ripe whites if these sorts of dishes are being eaten; otherwise, stick to lighter styles.

• After the starters, a red is a must. If several different dishes have been ordered, choose from the versatile reds already mentioned as they will go well with most things. If you are all tucking into one thing – say, roast beef – then here's your chance to pick something more esoteric that makes a very good match; for example, a fine Australian Shiraz or Bordeaux blend.

• Towards the end of the main course, consider whether a sweet wine or a port is appropriate (this depends on whether diners are having dessert or cheese). Take a look the list again and choose either by the half-bottle or by the glass. Don't rule out sweet Madeiras, sherries or sparklers at the end of the meal.

# wines for special occasions

Those organising a wedding or other special occasion tend to fall prey to acute 'wine worry'. After all, the day will be ruined if the wines aren't perfect, won't it? Well, no, actually – most people are far too busy chatting and dancing to care much about what's in their glass.

Fussy old uncle Henry is far more likely to notice a poor wine when he is relaxing at home on his own or dining out, and actually giving some serious thought to his food and drink. But it is understandable that wedding planners, or anyone organising a special event, want everything to be spot-on – especially if a lot of money is being spent on the booze. Here are some tips for those with the jitters:

• Choose easy-drinking, soft, fruity styles of wine – not ones with 'difficult' characteristics. Aim to buy crowd-pleasers that slip down easily, and don't be tempted to show off with unusual styles. This is not the moment for a heavily tannic red, a spine-tinglingly tart white, a weird dessert wine or a peculiar red sparkler.

• Don't be tempted by a seriously cut-price, unknown wine from a discount warehouse (unless you get a good taste of it first). It could well be a dud. Trade up from bargain basement, sticking to the medium price brackets for something palatable and safe.

• Let's cut to the chase: safe bets for whites include New Zealand Sauvignon Blanc, premium South African Chenin Blanc, Sauvignon-Sémillon blends from the southwest of France, Vin de Pays des Côtes de Gascogne, and soft Australian Semillon-Chardonnay blends for newer-wines fans. Reds might include Chilean Merlot, decent Beaujolais-Villages, southern-hemisphere Pinot Noir, Argentinian Bonarda, and Southern Italian reds from Puglia.

• You do *not* need to buy frighteningly expensive Champagne for a big event – in fact, you don't have to have Champagne at all. If you do splash out, go for a reliable big name or a cheaper Champers that you have tasted in advance. Do beware of pricey vintage Champagnes that are not mature (they should be at least six years old). Remember that plenty of non-European sparklers, French *crémants* and Spanish cavas will go down just as well as inferior Champagnes – often for a fraction of the price.

• One idea is to buy a few bottles of fine Champagne for the toasts, and lots of cheaper fizz for the rest of the bash. Consider magnums as well.

• Make sure your fizz is *brut* (dry) – this is not the moment for sweet sparkling wine like Asti unless it is specifically to serve with a celebration cake.

• Make sure the wines are relatively young and fresh, and be sure to have chilled the whites and sparklers before serving. Warm wine will taste horrible, especially in an over-crowded, over-heated event.

• Consider putting a bottle of port or dessert wine on each table if you are providing a big feast that includes dessert. This will look generous and interesting to guests who expect only the standard red and white!

• If booking a venue where you are required to serve the house wines, be sure to taste them well in advance of your event. If they are poor, say so and ask for something different, or put in a request to bring your own wines. Expect a charge for this, but do negotiate if it seems unreasonable.

• Trust your instincts. Get in few different bottles for a mini-tasting in advance and pick one or two favourites. Good luck!

# index

**Picture credits**
Special photography by William Reavell

**13** Scope/Jacques Guillard; **15** Cephas/Mick Rock; **16 above** Corbis/© Corbis Sygma/Terres du Sud; **16 below** Corbis/Charles O'Rear; **21 above** Cephas/Kevin Judd; **21 below** Cephas/Andy Christodolo; **23** Cephas/Mick Rock; **55** Cephas/Kjell Karlsson; **67** Cephas/Mick Rock; **75** Cephas/Micky Martin; **83** Scope/Jacques Guillard; **95** Cephas/Mick Rock; **109** Cephas/Mick Rock; **114** Scope/Jacques Guillard; **135** Cephas/Mick Rock; **149** Cephas/Mick Rock; **164** Cephas/Mick Rock; **171** The Interior Archive/Fritz von der Schulenburg/designer Julia Twigg; **172** www.elizabethwhiting.com/Mark Luscombe-White.

**Acknowledgements**
Many thanks to the team at Quadrille, especially Jane, Lisa and Helen, for all their hard work, expertise and enthusiasm. Thanks as well to my agent Martine Carter, Jamie Ambrose for proofreading, and all in the Sainsbury's wine department for their help. Most of all, I'd like to thank my wonderful husband Ian Acheson for putting up with me while this book took shape.